I dedicate this book to my partner and wife,
Jacqueline Allen-Doucot,
who has been my ally, mentor, and coconspirator
in the struggle for a better world
for twenty-five loving years
—CHRISTOPHER J. DOUCOT

For Bella
—SHANNON CRAIGO-SNELL

Contents

Foreword by Timothy P. Shriver ix

Introduction 1

1. Understanding the Struggles for LGBTQ
   Equality and Racial Justice 19
2. Getting Ready to Be an Ally 51
3. Resources for Being an Ally 71
4. Concrete Steps 95
5. Examples to Follow 120

An Invitation 140

Notes 142

For Further Study 153

Acknowledgments 156

Foreword

When I was a young teacher at Hillhouse High School in the mid-80s, I was asked to organize an after-school group to help young male students develop leadership skills and become positive role models in the school.

Hillhouse was a wonderful school, full of teenagers who were raucous and curious, oppositional and needy, angry and tender, studious and disengaged—just like all teenagers. Like all teenagers, they were focused on life's big questions like "who will I date?" and "how will I survive in this big tough world?" and "where do I belong?" And, of course, they were focused on math, science, languages, social studies, and the arts too.

To the rest of our city, however, Hillhouse students were known by different labels: they were seen as poor and African American; as likely to drop out or get in trouble with the law; as "at risk" and risky. People I knew from suburban communities were intimidated by Hillhouse. "You work there?" they asked incredulously. "Aren't you afraid?"

I wasn't but I could understand their view. I was keenly aware of the problems that racked the community and of racism in the city and the nation. I understood the deeply ingrained patterns of discrimination and segregation that led whites to fear African Americans. I watched as media outlets offered story after story of violence and disaster in New Haven. I realized that the white perception of my students was governed by negative forces.

But I also knew that their perception was wrong. After just a few short years of work, I had become mesmerized by the charm and intelligence and authenticity of my students. They were teaching me as much as I was teaching them. I was at Hillhouse to do my part to offer them real opportunity, but I was also there to fight the racism that blocked so many of their hopes and possibilities. I wanted to help them, but I also wanted to change the culture that in so many ways was hurting them.

For all these reasons it was ordinary for me to accept the responsibility of creating an after-school group whose aim was not only to intensify support for my students but also to empower them to be visible agents of positive service to the community. So I recruited a few of the most challenging young men at the school and asked them to help me launch an after-school club. They agreed, and after a few initial meetings, we had attracted about twenty students and named ourselves the Young Men's Leadership Group. The members were all African American, all male, and all "at risk." They were also smart, funny, raw, generous, and searching.

The group met once a week. Some days, we talked about chemistry homework and writing papers for teachers; other days we talked about gangs and fights. Some days, we ate pizza and discussed girlfriend problems; other days, we made our way into the community to clean up streets or to paint the house of an indigent neighbor. Our goal was simple: to support one another in becoming the leaders we each believed we could be.

Word of our group got around the school and the neighborhood because some of the guys weren't the types who were usually perceived as "leaders" and because it seemed unusual for a group of male Hillhouse students to roam the school and the streets smiling, laughing, and serving others. Members of the "L," as we came to call ourselves, didn't miraculously become angels, but they did listen to each other and came steadily to the realization that despite their surroundings and in the face of massive obstacles, they were smart and strong and capable of being sources of positive energy for themselves and others too.

On one occasion, I was contacted by an administrator from our New Haven neighbor, Yale College, with a request: Would I bring the "Young Men's Leadership Group" to speak on campus? This was something of a shock. Hillhouse students—particularly young men—were not typical guest speakers at Yale. But our group took the invitation to heart, and five members volunteered to enter the ivy covered buildings at Yale's Old Campus and share their stories. Unknowingly, we were about to experience what Chris Doucot and Shannon Craigo-Snell describe as a moment where grace—"the unarmed gift of being able to be honest"— broke through in a conversation about race.

The event opened with our five young men sitting in front of a packed Yale classroom of eager undergraduates. Each young man opened with a brief statement: "I'm Doug and I live in Dixwell, and I'd like to go to college to be a teacher"; or "I'm Todd and I live in Newhallville, and I'd like to go to college to be a lawyer"; and so on. One of the members described our group and what it was about. Another described our goal of raising enough money to buy jackets for seniors who would be graduating. Another described a dance we were planning for the school and our strategy for keeping it safe.

The Yale moderator then began with questions. "What can Yale students to do help you?" was the first.

The "L" students sat stone faced. Silence.

"Let me ask it another way. Yale students want to volunteer in the community and serve. What should they do?"

Silence again. I fidgeted. The scene was uncomfortable. Hundreds of highly accomplished, elite white students from around the world were sitting and staring at five African American high school students from New Haven's poorest neighborhoods almost as though they were on display. "This was a bad idea," I thought to myself as the silence persisted. I wanted to jump in but knew it was up to the guys to decide what to say.

Finally, one of the L members spoke up. "Well I don't know much about Yale students, but most of the time when I see them they don't know what's going on and they act like they know everything."

Silence.

Then another member of the group chimed in. "To tell you the truth, I don't want no help from you. I just don't want you in my way. You don't need to come into my neighborhood."

The moderator could see that the conversation wasn't going in the direction he'd wanted and tried to shift it back. "Are you saying that you don't want any support to achieve your goals?"

"I didn't say that, man. I mean y'all got everything here and you all talk about wanting to do this and that and what not. But every time I see y'all come around wanting to help, you're all up on this big white horse and acting like you know everything and treating everybody like shit. I'm not gonna lie: I do need a lot of help, but not from some asshole who looks down on me."

Then another Hillhouse student chimed in: "That's right but I'm gonna put it another way: you know, people: we can get along together and all, but y'all just gotta come down from y'all's white horse and meet us on the level. You know what I'm saying?"

His voice lightened.

"I mean just meet us like eye to eye and you could help us a lot. You know what I'm saying?"

After another tense silence, one Yale student started to applaud. And then a rousing ovation followed. And when the room quieted down, the discussion became lively and animated. "Eye to eye" was the topic, not "helping" or "serving." Coming down off of white horses became the subject of discussion, not tutoring or college preparation. All of a sudden, a couple hundred people between the ages of fourteen and twenty-two were talking about the "problem of the twentieth century" in the United States of America: the vast gap between white and black created by racism, the misunderstandings that so often distort any attempts to bridge it, and the painful honesty needed to begin to heal it.

The class went on for more than an hour with the Leadership Group members putting it all on the table. The world was unfair, racist, and infuriating to them. They were often ready to give up. Their parents worked multiple jobs and never had enough. School was boring and didn't help anyone. They told the Yale students not to come to certain neighborhoods because so many of their friends would rather beat them up than do homework. They told them how much they wanted to do something positive, how they were trying to do better even in the face of so much disappointment.

At the close, one of the L members shifted gears. "You know, at least we're here." He looked at his fellow Hillhouse guys and said, "look at us, y'all. We're members of the L and we're gonna get jackets this year and we're at Yale. And you know a lot of folks never expected us to be here and you know these Yale folk are listening to us. They're listening to *us*! We should be proud, you know what I'm saying? I'm proud to be here with y'all and that's real to me."

I believe this was the first time that those Yale students heard Hillhouse students tell the honest truth about poverty, race, and privilege. And I know it was a first for the Hillhouse students, too, because they told me. As we walked back to Hillhouse and talked about the experience, everyone laughed and repeated some of the priceless lines and kept replaying the questions and how they had handled them. They were beaming. They had told their truth to the people from Yale, who represented so many of the frustrations of their lives. It was liberating.

Alas, the visit of the Young Men's Leadership Group to the

Yale campus didn't solve the racial problems of the United States. Some of those leadership group young men went on to college, and some finished high school. But some ended up in jail too: the odds against them didn't change much because of our group. Maybe we beat them a little but not enough. The larger forces at work in the United States were still mostly destructive for African American young men. It was both heartbreaking and infuriating to be a part of the system then. No matter how hard teachers tried and no matter how hard students tried, the deck was stacked. A few made it, but far too few. And for the rest, there was mostly tragedy. The conditions for people of color in cities like New Haven were, and remain, an outrageous indictment of our country.

But long odds aren't a reason not to try—once and for all—to bridge the long painful gap that separates people of color from white folk in the United States of America. And this book is a good place to launch that effort to try anew. Chris Doucot and Shannon Craigo-Snell have taken a risky first step: they've written a book that asks us all to recognize the enormous injustice of our system, to delve into the awkward and tense conversations needed to expose racism, to own the roles we have each played in its perpetuation, and to make honest and significant efforts to end it—urgently.

If there is only one lesson to keep in mind as you read this book and think about its implications for your life, I suggest it is this: Chris Doucot and Shannon Craigo-Snell make it very clear that we made the system we have, and we can unmake it too. Racism runs deep in the United States—as deep as the rivers that Langston Hughes celebrated in his great poem, "The Negro Speaks of Rivers." But no matter how deep they might be, rivers flow. Everything is in motion. Our foremothers and forefathers own responsibility for the poison of racism that is in our midst today, but others worked hard to cleanse it too. Countless and usually nameless citizens gave themselves and their lives for equality, some hanging from trees, some marching across bridges, some just taking the time to listen and try to understand.

We owe ourselves more than the status quo lest we also pass on a legacy of injustice and anguish. And make no mistake: this is not just an issue for people of color; it is also an issue for all of us. Nelson Mandela reminded us that freedom isn't just for those in chains. It is also about all of us learning to live in a way that respects the "freedom and dignity of others." "I am not truly free if I am taking away someone else's freedom, just as surely as I am not free when my freedom is taken from me. The oppressed and the oppressor alike are robbed of their humanity."[1] Racism is a scourge that has brutalized the lives of millions of African Americans, but we are all damaged by its lies and its horrors. No one escapes the brutality. And everyone will be better when we end its stranglehold on all our lives.

This book is an important place to start—a call to listen once more to the words of the prophets and by listening to them, allow ourselves to be changed. And the change that we need perhaps more than any other is simply this: that we might each and together be willing to give something real and meaningful to our children, to our country, and to our future: dignity for all.

No matter how high the obstacle, we must take the big risk. Wherever we are, we can come down off our white horses. And when we do, we can meet each other eye to eye. And there, in those moments of seeing, we can begin to chart our way into a more just and joyful America. It can't come fast enough.

Timothy P. Shriver

Introduction

Another video is in the news today. Another incident of brutality against a black person, this time a "student resource officer" flipping a high school student and her desk over, then dragging her out of her chair and slamming her to the ground. The video shows a quiet classroom—no chaos, no danger—until deputy Ben Fields seizes the petite girl sitting at her school desk. The young girl was arrested for "disturbing school," apparently by having her phone out during class.[1] Tellingly, a classmate who recorded the incident on her cell phone and protested the violence was also taken into custody. This incident happened at Spring Valley High School in Columbia, South Carolina, but we know it could have happened almost anywhere in the United States. We know this because there is another video every week in a different location. We saw the video of Eric Garner in New York, Michael Brown's body in Missouri, Tamir Rice in Ohio, Eric Harris and Terence Crutcher in Oklahoma, Jerame Reid in New Jersey, Walter Scott in South Carolina, Philando Castile in Minnesota. We saw the video of officers assaulting young black people at a pool party in Texas and beating a sixteen-year-old black boy in California. We saw the headlines about Freddie Gray in Maryland, Tony Robinson in Wisconsin, Rumain Brisbon in Arizona, Ezell Ford in

California, John Crawford III in Ohio. The list goes on, and the evidence mounts that something has gone terribly wrong in the United States.

Many Americans watch the latest cell phone video with sadness, bafflement, and outrage. For those who are white, the mixture of emotions often includes questions and conflicts about how to respond faithfully. We suspect that our religious and spiritual lives mean something about the roles we should take in the current movement for racial justice in America. We feel a sense of calling toward a better, more just way of living together.

But how? There isn't a road map for well-meaning white people who want to help create racial justice. And quite frankly, it is more complicated than some other imperatives for a virtuous life. We know that we are supposed to share our money and resources with the poor. We might not do it as much as we should, but at least we know it is within the realm of possibility. But when it comes to racism, the way forward is less obvious. As white people, aren't we part of the problem? We are constantly reminded that racism benefits us. While we could give away our money, we cannot give away our whiteness.

And then there is fear. We are afraid of the fallout if we engage our cousins, neighbors, or coworkers on issues of race. We are also afraid we will say the wrong thing, offend someone, or simply stand out and be embarrassed. All of us have seen, in person or in the media, a well-intentioned white person say or do the wrong thing and then get called racist. Sometimes it seems like any effort a white person makes to help the situation will be misconstrued. We have also seen instances when a white person attempts to be helpful but then makes a misstep. His work on behalf of people of color quickly becomes a way of boosting his own importance. He assumes that his role in every effort is to lead it, unwittingly putting a white man in charge once again. Afraid to say the wrong thing, it seems safer to stay silent.

We can even pretend that our silence is a kind of high-minded neutrality. There are many sides to every story. We imagine that we can inhabit a neutral position that does not support either side of a contested issue. Such neutrality is an illusion. While considering and appreciating different perspectives on any issue is an important step in making thoughtful choices, stopping at "seeing both sides" of a moral issue is irresponsible. In a situation of injustice or oppression, neutrality sustains injustice. Archbishop Desmond Tutu states it plainly: "If you are neutral in situations of injustice, you have chosen the side of the oppressor."[2] Whatever its roots or justifications, silence also speaks. From a jail cell in Birmingham, Rev. Dr. Martin Luther King Jr. pointedly responded to criticism from apparently sympathetic and well-intentioned white clergy that the work and words of civil rights activists were "unwise and untimely." King wrote, "We will have to repent . . . not merely for the hateful words and actions of the bad people but for the appalling silence of the good people."[3] When those who have a modicum of power are silent in regard to injustice, this is a tacit acceptance and support of oppression.

The word "ally" is currently used to refer to someone working for justice with a group other than the group with which they identify. This term is imperfect and problematic for reasons that will be addressed later; but for now, this is the vocabulary at hand. The question is, How to be an ally in the struggle for racial justice? How can we do this well, in ways that don't cause more harm than good?

Many white people in the United States—particularly those who are middle-class—have found that stepping into the role of ally in the movement for LGBTQ liberation is easier than stepping into a similar role in the movement for racial justice. Furthermore, the work of allies seems to have been decidedly helpful for LGBTQ activism. In many ways, the United States has moved forward quickly on issues of LGBTQ rights while we appear to be moving backwards, or are at the very least stuck in the past, regarding racial justice. There has been remarkable success in changing attitudes, laws, and policies regarding LGBTQ rights. Part of this success stems from getting straight people on board as allies. On the path toward understanding how to best be allies in the struggle for racial justice, we will briefly explore the role of allies in LGBTQ activism. This will introduce *allyship* and provide a comparison from which to discern why it has been so difficult for allies to function as well in antiracist efforts.

We are convinced that there are many people in the United States who care deeply about racial injustice and feel called to a better world but perhaps do not know where to begin. This book offers an introduction to some of the issues and practical guidelines for how to be an ally in the struggle against racism. The wisdom on these pages is largely gleaned from activists and allies who are involved in the struggle for racial justice, for LGBTQ equality, or both. Several activist advisors have contributed to this project by giving on-the-ground perspectives about the roles that people of privilege can and can't play effectively. Insights from these stories help us understand how we can form alliances in struggles for justice. Furthermore, they are shaped by the worldview of our particular religious tradition, Christianity. The conversation in these pages is not always comfortable or cheery. However, it will prepare you to engage in conversations and concrete actions to foster racial justice in our communities.

This text focuses on antiblack racism. This is only one form of racism among many. Asian Americans, Latino/as/x, native peoples, and many others experience distinct and deadly forms of oppression. We do not deny these forms of racism nor do we imagine that they are identical to, completely separate from, or less important than antiblack racism. Our focus draws a fairly arbitrary margin in order to more clearly examine the role of allies in the work for racial justice. We sincerely hope that reading this book will spur you to read other books that examine the struggles of other racialized and oppressed groups.

This book is an introduction, and an imperfect one at that. Its authors are not the foremost experts on racism or heterosexism, although the footnotes can lead you to some of those. We are simply Christians who have, in various ways, been involved in struggles for justice for many years. Christopher Doucot is a straight, white man who cofounded the Catholic Worker House in Hartford, Connecticut. For twenty-five years, he has lived in an impoverished black and brown community, sharing his home with neighbors and strangers and engaging in activism at a local, national, and international level. Chris is a New Englander who strongly opposes Manhattan clam chowder. Shannon Craigo-Snell is a straight, white woman who teaches theology at a seminary in Kentucky. Over the years, she has been involved in community organizing, peacemaking, and the Black Lives Matter movement. A West Virginia native, Shannon is raising her children on beans and cornbread.

As white, straight people, we understand that this work can be tricky, and it can be hard to know where to begin. The same is true with the writing of this book. For some, it will be too simplistic; for others, it will be too challenging; and for still others, it will seem like hubris for the two of us to address these topics at all. However, while we are white and straight, we are also Christian, and we cannot witness the harm done by structural oppression, and individual acts of prejudice, without attempting to change things. Our limitations are not an excuse for inaction.

This book is intended for practical use. Our primary sources of insight are not textbooks, but stories from activists. However, there a few concepts that are central to all that is to follow and therefore worth defining here. The first of these is structural oppression.

STRUCTURAL OPPRESSION

Racism is a form of structural oppression. The most common way to think about racism is to imagine a person who harbors ill will against people of color or who believes stereotypes about people of color. However, this view of racism is profoundly unhelpful. Such discriminatory attitudes are not racism; they are prejudice and bigotry. Racism is not merely a matter of individual feelings and beliefs but also a matter of systemic oppression. To understand racism in America we need to take a step back and acknowledge that there are indeed social systems operating in our midst. We are reluctant to do this in America, because we hold dear an ethos of individualism. This reverence for the power of the individual is deeply embedded in our national psyche and reflected in our myths (see Horatio Alger and the belief that those who work hard succeed), our heroes (Superman), our archetypes (the Cowboy), and our villains (Bernie Madoff). In America we want to believe that every success was individually earned and every failure is the result of individual shortcoming.

However, our individual lives play out within a framework of social systems. To get a glimpse of this, let's consider the transportation system.[4] In twenty-first-century America, the transportation system is car-centered, car-dominated, and car-identified, which functions to the advantage of people who own cars. Sitting in traffic every rush hour you might not recognize how this system privileges you. If you don't own a car, and don't live in one of the few American cities with adequate public transportation, then the reality that our transportation system is car-dominated, car-identified, and car-centered confronts every aspect of your daily life. If you get around by bicycle, you use roads and signals that don't work for you. It is nearly impossible to turn left at a busy intersection and interstates prohibit bicycles all together. If you cycle to work, it is unlikely there will be a shower waiting for you; but if you drive, then there will probably be a garage or parking lot.

Many poor people are pedestrians and consumers of public transportation. They walk to and from bus stops to get where they are going. Walking limits employment opportunities to within walking distance. You can take a bus to the suburbs, but most suburbanites have cars, so bus stops are few and far between and even sidewalks are scarce. If you depend on the bus, this dictates where you live, work, go to the doctor, and go out for entertainment. Relying on the bus limits not only where you can work but also when, because your work hours need to conform to bus schedules. Think about grocery shopping without a car. Consider how hard it would be to buy frozen foods on a summer day or how the amount you purchase depends on how much you can fit and push in a collapsible cart or carry on the bus. Some cities have zoning requirements that mandate a certain number of parking spaces for major supermarkets. This makes it difficult for supermarkets to open up downtown, so the wide selection and cheap prices are often found in the suburbs because, once again, the system is car-centered, car-dominated, and car-identified. In many cities, driver's licenses are needed for other activities, including opening a bank account and even voting. While you can get an alternative government issued photo ID, these are most often issued by the Department of Motor Vehicles. If you don't have a car, you have to walk, bike, or ride the bus to the DMV before you can exercise basic rights of American citizenship.

Not only do those of us with cars not have these worries, we don't know they are worries at all for those without cars. If we have the privilege of car ownership, the system works to our advantage. It is easy not to notice that there is a system at all.

Racism is like this. The United States of America was created and structured under the influence of white supremacy, so the economic, political, and social structures of this country are white-dominated, white-identified, and white-centered.[5] The United States was built for white people in the same way that twentieth-century American cities were built for car owners. If you are white, it is difficult to see all of the difficulties faced by those who are not. It is much, much easier to not notice the system at all. Because racism is a system, it flourishes in the absence of systemic analysis: in other words, if we can keep all our conversations about racism focused on *individual* prejudices, motives, or intent, then we do not notice the system at all.

With this newfound understanding of our transportation system operating as a system of privilege for car owners, perhaps you are inspired to give up your car in order to be in solidarity with those who don't own cars. Aside from the benefit to your health and the environment, will giving up your car end "carism"? Obviously not, because the system that privileges owning a car would not be affected. Giving up your car will not increase bus service, build bike paths, or pave sidewalks in the suburbs. In the same way, for an individual to imagine that her antiracist work is finished because she does not personally hold prejudiced views is a deception.

To end car privilege would require that system to be replaced. If we flash back a hundred years we can see that this is not farfetched. In 1915 we had a system of transportation that was rail-identified, rail-centered, and rail-dominated. In this era the trolley lines on the east coast were so extensive that one could travel from Florida to Maine by trolley! The demise of this system coincided with the rise of the automobile and a variety of unacknowledged public subsidies that built the car-privileging system of today.[6] This system has also reinforced racial segregation in America.[7] "Car-ism" is the result of public policy decisions. This means the privileges of "car-ism" can be mitigated by new public policy decisions. In the same way, racism is a socially constructed reality upheld by public policy decisions that reinforced white supremacy. While seeing the systemic view of racism can be overwhelming, there is hope in knowing that it is not natural or inevitable. People made this; people can unmake it.

Whereas giving up one's car doesn't change the system of "car-ism," it does make one experientially aware of the frustrations, limited opportunities, and injustice of being car-less in a car-dominated, car-identified, car-centered society. This epiphany should not be dismissed. If our employers, doctors, teachers, and social workers all drive to work, will they sympathize with the car-less when they are late or miss an appointment because the bus was late? Will legislators who haven't ridden a bus since grade school not only sponsor but advocate for increased funding for public transportation? The conversation on transportation is dominated by those who own cars. For the system to be altered, the conversation needs to be challenged by the voices of those without cars. Furthermore, the harm done by systemic "car-ism" needs to be recognized by those who have cars.

The benefits of being white in a white-centered and white-dominated society are often hard for those who accrue them to notice. We have always had these benefits, so they seem natural. In recent years, these benefits have been called "white privilege" and a great deal of work has been done to help white people see and understand this reality.[8] While we use this term, we do so sparingly for two reasons. First, focusing on white privilege can be a way to continue to speak primarily about white people. This is not the intent of those who use this term but rather an unfortunate pitfall. Second, some of the benefits that accrue to white people are not privileges. Easy access to voting, quality public education, and fair treatment by law enforcement are not privileges. They are rights.

There are several forms of structural oppression, including racism, sexism, heterosexism, and classism. Each of these forms benefits the group that is considered normal or standard. That group can be identified as the dominant culture. The group that is not centered can be called marginalized, as they are pushed to the margins of society. Most of us fit within the dominant group in some ways and are marginalized in others. For example, a poor white person is part of the dominant white culture but marginalized as a poor person. Often, a person experiences two or more forms of structural oppression. A poor white woman has to deal with classism and sexism. A transgender black person has to deal with heterosexism and racism. These multiple forms of oppression do not just add up like building blocks. Instead, they interact with each other like dangerous chemicals. Heterosexism, sexism, classism, and racism do not just exist side-by-side, they also influence and strengthen each other. This is called *intersectionality*.[9] Although it is useful to look at various "-isms" individually, we must also attend to the ways they overlap, intersect, and interact.

Intersectional oppression happens in a very basic way: becoming accustomed to ranking one group of people over others in regard to one form of identity (such as race) makes it easier for us to think in a similar hierarchical pattern in regard to another form of identity (such as gender and sexuality). It also happens in more complicated ways. For instance, in nineteenth-century America, a "true woman" was supposed to be pious, pure, domestic, and submissive. This ideal was unattainable for enslaved black women who were forced to work in the field and subject to rape by the slaveholders. Enslaved black women were then seen as less than true women. This made it easier for a society that, on one level, told gentlemen to protect and honor white, upper-class women and, on another level, to physically exploit black, poor, and immigrant women.[10]

GRACE

Another concept that informs all the pages that follow is grace. There are many ways of understanding the spiritual dimensions of our lives, including different religious traditions and ethical frameworks. As we address these issues from a Christian perspective, the notion of grace is key.

It would be easier to choose not to see the oppressive systems that surround us. It would be more comfortable to deny our participation in these systems. And yet, the grace of God pulls us to recognize the systems that cause such harm.

Grace refers to the free, unearned gift of God's own self that God gives to us in many ways. God does not remain distant and uninvolved with humanity but rather persistently loves us and calls us into loving relationships with God and one another. While the idea that grace can make us see painful things might seem counterintuitive, it is actually a profound truth of Christian theology. It is because we glimpse God's love that we know we fall short of loving well. It is because we taste the goodness of God that we realize how bitter human enmity can be. It is because we recognize others as children of God that we cry out when they are brutalized. The grace of God reveals what human community ought to be, placing oppressive realities in stark relief.

On a personal level, the grace of God undoes our own pretensions. When we know that God loves us, we can stop trying to impress God or win God over. We can let our guard down about all the ways we fail and falter. The most arrogant, self-centered, conceited people are often those with the greatest insecurities. Without a strong sense of self, the arrogant man needs to convince himself that he is important by convincing those around him. In contrast, a man who knows his own worth does not need to brag or boast. A woman who fears appearing foolish will argue her point to the bitter end; while a woman who knows she is intelligent can admit when she is mistaken without suffering a loss of self. The grace and love of God secure a sense of self in the Christian, which makes it possible for Christians to admit our shortcomings, confess our sins, and even recognize our own complicity in systems of oppression.

The grace of God also undoes our self-abasement. When we trust that God loves us, we can no longer imagine we are unlovable or incapable of goodness. We are not permitted to shy away from our own potential, freedom, and power. There are many people in the world who imagine they are not good enough, important enough, or strong enough to make a difference in the world. When faced with the enormity of structural oppression, we can become overwhelmed and morally paralyzed. Too often, the awareness that no one individual can fix the whole problem leads us to absolve ourselves from even trying. The grace of God can secure a sense of self, both challenging and enabling the Christian to affirm her own value, potential, and power.

These two positions—pretension and self-abasement—are two sides of the same coin. Both are postures taken up by human beings who do not recognize that they are loved by God. Our worth and value is already given to us by God in grace, but we don't believe it. In our denial of our God-given worth, we sometimes struggle to justify our own existence. The theological term for this is pride. Alternatively, we might deny our God-given worth by failing to live into our calling as Christians. The theological term for this is sloth. Both pride and sloth are denials of God's grace and love.[11]

When we accept God's love, it can have an enormous effect on us. As noted theologian Howard Thurman writes, "awareness of being a child of God tends to stabilize the ego and results in a new courage, fearlessness, and power." Such awareness establishes "the ground of personal dignity" and affords the Christian a form of humility that cannot be humiliated. The awareness of being a child of God does not remove all obstacles from a Christian's path, but it does allow her to perceive her own strengths and possibilities much more clearly. Thurman continues, "If a man's ego has been stabilized, resulting in a sure grounding of his sense of personal worth and dignity, then he is in a position to appraise his own intrinsic powers, gifts, talents, and abilities."[12] These words were originally written for the benefit of those who are oppressed or disinherited, for those who have their backs against the wall. Yet this wisdom is also useful to those of us who have various kinds of privilege.

For many white people, learning the history of white supremacy can be extremely threatening. It is difficult to learn that the category of whiteness has always been a justification for harm to others. In this regard it does not make sense to be proud of being white. Does this mean we should be ashamed of who we are? No. Instead, it means we should question whether or not race is the primary category we want to use in identifying ourselves. We cannot opt out of whiteness; we will still benefit from racism in many ways, and denying this helps sustain the system of white supremacy. However, we can acknowledge the socially constructed categories of race and the system of white supremacy as circumstances we were born into and therefore must navigate. Instead of navigating these circumstances as people whose identities are secured by whiteness, we can steer through these turbulent waters as people whose identities rest in other categories. Some antiracist authors suggest that white people in the United States should reclaim the identities claimed by their ancestors who first came to America, such as Italian or Irish. This pushes back against the construction of whiteness. For others, claiming a more local, current identity might be meaningful, perhaps for an Appalachian or a New Englander. For those who are Christian, our primary identity rests in Jesus Christ. This can and should recalibrate our posture toward all the other identities that are put on us. This Christian identity is both gift and task. We are *called* beloved children of God, and we are *called to* justice, mercy, and humility. The work of justice and the grace that makes it possible are given together.

In Romans 12, the apostle Paul speaks of the grace that has been given to him and entreats his readers to live according to grace. Romans 12 is a guide to being gracious: "Contribute to the needs of the saints, practice hospitality. Bless those who persecute you; bless, and do not curse. Rejoice with those who rejoice, and weep with those who weep. Be of the same mind toward one another. Do not be haughty, but associate with the lowly. Do not pretend to be wiser than you are." (Rom. 13–16 MEV). This is the task of an ally.

WHAT IS AN ALLY?

An ally is a person who is a member of the dominant culture in at least one respect who chooses to engage in work for justice regarding precisely that characteristic in which they are part of the dominant culture. A straight person who works for LGBTQ rights, a white person who works against racism, a middle-class person who fights systems that create poverty, and so forth.

Most important, an ally does this by standing with, supporting, and working with people who are not part of the dominant culture in this regard. They make common cause with those who are marginalized. Rev. Josh Pawelek, a Unitarian Universalist minister who is involved in Black Lives Matter, movements for LGBTQ equality, and other struggles for justice, says that the key to becoming an ally is that "people of privilege and dominant culture identity make themselves accountable to people of marginalized and oppressed identity in the struggle for justice. Call it allyship. Call it solidarity. Call it partnership. Call it beloved community. There are a lot of names for it."

The prevalence of the term "ally" emerged through the struggle for LGBTQ equality in the latter part of the twentieth century. A straight person who identified as an "ally" indicated that they did not believe in or accept discrimination of LGBTQ people. Students organized groups known as Gay/Straight Alliances (GSAs) to provide safe spaces for LGBTQ youth and to advocate for equality. In many ways, the efficacy of allies in the movement for LGBTQ equality has made this the term used most often for members of dominant cultures who work for justice alongside those who are marginalized.

However, the term—and the concept—is not without difficulties. In general, allies have been much more problematic in working to end antiblack racism. While simply declaring oneself an ally or one's dorm room a safe space truly did foster acceptance of LGBTQ people, simply declaring oneself an ally for people of color is not helpful. It does not address the systems and structures of racism. Jessica Stewart, an activist and author, writes, "Race seems really different because of its centrality to all systems of oppression in America. White supremacy is so woven into the economic and political fabric of our country that engaging as an ally in the struggle for racial justice is essential, but also difficult and perhaps problematic in unique ways."

Amy Plantinga Pauw, a scholar who has been very active in the movement for LGBTQ equality, notes that the term "ally" is, "a military image that seems to divide people into allies and enemies, and it seems more problematic in struggles for racial justice" than in work for LGBTQ equality. Rev. Valerie Bridgeman—a preacher, professor, and activist—is also troubled by the military nature of the term. Military alliances are strategic and variable. She writes, "it allows for the 'ally' to come in and out of the fray, not to have to participate when there's no clear gain for them."

Several of the activists who advised this project mentioned that allies in the struggle for racial justice can choose to opt in or opt out at different times. Dr. Ludger Viefhues-Bailey, a former activist and current professor, notes that "the ally has the option to step out of companionship with the minoritized person."

Rev. Dr. Lewis Brogdon, activist and scholar, notes that this choice to be in or out of the struggle is another benefit of being part of the dominant culture. He writes, "An ally is one who intentionally sides with marginalized communities in the fight against injustice but even that act is an extension of privilege because one has the choice to do so or not. An ally always has privilege and the choice to act against or to participate with injustice. This can be a limitation in the term. It can seduce allies into thinking that they can deny their privilege." Community activist Rex Fowler reads this imbalance from the other side, noting that the term ally implies that the marginalized "person apparently needs something/someone to advocate for them, whereas I, as the ally, don't necessarily need anyone." Several activists have suggested other terms that imply more shared risk and partnership, including "accomplices" and "coconspirators."[13]

Although there are problems with the term, Rev. Nyle Fort, who is an activist and community organizer, reminds us that the work is more important than the terminology and that, "those who want to be in solidarity are actually re-centering themselves by focusing more on what to call themselves than what they're called to do." With his wise counsel in mind, we take the word "ally," imperfect as it is, to gesture toward relationships of shared struggle that cross boundaries of dominant cultures and social locations.

The chapters that follow fall into three sections: historical, theological, and practical. In the historical section, we begin with a brief overview of the struggle for LGBTQ equality, including the social construction of sexual identity, the history of structural oppression of people who are LGBTQ, and the role of allies in the movement. Then we address racism in the same pattern: social construction, history of structural oppression, and the role of allies. Our hope is that this chapter will serve as a first step in understanding these ideas and a positive example of how allies can be useful.

The theological section begins with a quick survey of the various ways that the Bible describes God's intention for the world as one of justice and love. This is the particular shape of a Christian sense of a higher calling. Then we will address a specific problem that arises when white people apprehend racial injustice: white guilt. We argue that the categories of innocence and guilt are simply not suited to the realities of structural oppression. They lead us into a cul-de-sac of defensiveness and paralysis. Fortunately, Christian theology offers a different set of categories that help us both to understand and to struggle against systemic oppression.

Our activist advisers take center stage in the practical section of the book, which begins with concrete advice for how to proceed in working for racial justice. Quotations from these activists will not be cited; they all reference personal interviews with the authors.

The final chapter of the book highlights four allies whose work inspires us and leads the way.

ACTIVIST ADVISORS TO THIS BOOK

The Rev. Dr. Marilyn McCord Adams[†] was a priest, theologian, and philosopher who was active in the struggle for LGBTQ equality.

Rev. Valerie Bridgeman, PhD, is a preacher, activist, and professor, who also served as a pastor for many years. She is involved in the Black Lives Matter movement, the struggle for LGBTQ equality, and efforts for fair wages.

Rev. Dr. Lewis Brogdon is a pastor and scholar who works for racial justice.

Rev. Nyle Fort is a writer, PhD student, and Black Lives Matter activist.

Rex Fowler is a community activist living in an impoverished, predominantly black and brown neighborhood. He also works on issues of racial and economic justice through his position as the executive director of the Hartford Community Loan Fund.[14]

The Rev. Wil Gafney, PhD, is an Episcopal priest, biblical scholar, and seminary professor. She is active in Black Lives Matter, interfaith work, and the struggle for LGBTQ equality. She works against white supremacy, racism, sexism, and heterosexism.

Jim Haber is an activist who is involved with work for Palestinian liberation, advocacy for the poor, immigrant rights, and peacemaking.

Frank O'Gorman describes himself as a "Queer Christian faith-based non-violent activist for social justice and peace."[15]

Dr. Amy Plantinga Pauw is a scholar and professor who is involved in the movement for LGBTQ equality and in efforts for racial justice.

Rev. Joshua M. Pawelek is a Unitarian Universalist minister who is involved in efforts for Black Lives Matter, LGBTQ equality, domestic workers' rights, environmental justice, and others.

Jessica Stewart is an activist and writer who is involved in the peace movement, the struggle for racial justice, and efforts for climate justice.

Ludger Viefhues-Bailey is a professor, college administrator, and former priest. He has been involved in HIV/AIDS activism and the struggle for LGBTQ equality. As a college administrator, he works to create campus-wide conversations on race and ethnicity.

DISCUSSION QUESTIONS

1. The authors suggest that it is better to think of injustice in terms of social systems than in terms of individual prejudice. How does that change what could be reasonably identified as racism?

2. Have you ever spent a period of time without access to a car? What did you discover that you didn't know before? What does that suggest about what those of us who are white know about the experiences of persons of color?

CHAPTER ONE

Understanding the Struggles for LGBTQ Equality and Racial Justice

In order to understand how to be an effective ally, we begin by looking at two movements for justice within the United States: the movement for LGBTQ equality and the struggle for racial justice. Examining the two side by side exposes some of the particular challenges to being an antiracist ally, challenges that are then addressed in following chapters.

LGBTQ ISSUES

The acronym "LGBTQ" stands for lesbian, gay, bisexual, transgender, and queer or questioning. Sometimes this is seen with an "I" at the end for intersex. In all its forms, this acronym intends to group together people whose sexual orientation and identity do not neatly conform to the standards of the dominant culture without collapsing them into one homogenous group. The name itself implies solidarity among different groups.[1] The terms within this acronym have to do with gender identity and sexual orientation.

SEXUAL ORIENTATION
AS A SOCIAL CONSTRUCT

More and more, scientists are discovering that anatomical and biological sex are far more complicated than a simple binary. Many people have both XX and XY chromosomes within different cells in their bodies. Current research indicates that as many as one person in a hundred might have chromosomes that do not conform to the binary understanding of gender as either male or female. Genetic differences make the standard gender binary seem even more inadequate, revealing our bodies to be far more complex.[2]

In spite of this fact, most of us are still taught by the culture in which we live that there are only two genders, and we must fit into one of them. We are also taught how to fit in—how to behave, dress, speak, move, and smile like a girl or like a boy. When historical and cultural forces create specific categories (such as male and female) and push us to live into these categories in specific ways (masculine and feminine behaviors), this is called *social construction.* Over long periods of time, and often without consciously choosing to do so, human cultures create categories through which we understand our world. Because this happens slowly on a large communal level, and without explicit plans, we don't notice it. We come into a world that already has categories and patterns, and we accept them as normal and natural. The expectations that history and culture have assigned to gender identity provide a prime example of social construction.

Sexual orientation, as we use the term today, includes elements of gender identity as well as sexual and romantic attraction. Sexual orientation is as complicated as gender identity. Various factors contribute to sexual orientation, including genetics, prenatal hormones, and environmental factors. There is no evidence to suggest that "sexual orientation can be taught or learned through social means."[3] Each person is the expert on their own sexual orientation—it is not something that can be decreed from the outside.

While people have always engaged in same-sex *activity*, the idea that sexual *orientation* is fundamental to a person's identity emerged much later. In many times and places, the gender to which one was sexually or romantically attracted did not determine how a person was categorized. No one was considered gay or lesbian. People were categorized in many ways—as merchants or servants or members of a particular family—and people within these categories sometimes loved people of the same sex. The categories of gay and lesbian had not yet been socially constructed.

As this has changed in more recent times, sexism has been a driving factor in constructing sexual orientation as an *identity*, rather than an *aspect* of someone's life, as men who engaged in same-sex love were perceived to be a threat to male dominance over women.[4] The enforcement of rigid, binary genders is a necessary element of the social power and privilege granted to men in the modern West. The primary fear in heterosexism is the blurring of lines that facilitate male dominance. Some straight men experience same-sex love between men as threatening their own sense of masculine identity. Other people see the very notion of being transgender as an assault on "natural" categories. LGBTQ equality challenges the idea that traditional categories of sex and gender are natural and unchanging.

Today, the word most commonly used to refer to the oppression of people who are LGBTQ is *homophobia*. While some individuals do display an irrational fear of LGBTQ persons, the term does not adequately describe the problem it is intended to address. While fear is part of the problem, the larger issue is that our culture is structured to benefit heterosexuals. As the United States is white dominant, white identified, and white centered, it is also straight-centered and straight-dominant. This structural and systemic feature of our culture is called *heterosexism*.

Steps Forward, Steps Back

Before the early twentieth century, people who found same-sex love generally kept it a secret from their friends and family. "Homosexuality" was seen by most Americans as a rare perversion, so many people were easily deceived; they never imagined that the two spinsters down the street were partners or that the confirmed bachelor actually had a fulfilling love life.[5] It was only with increased urbanization that LGBTQ people who had been isolated in rural and small town America began to form accepting communities. There were robust gay and lesbian communities in the United States and in parts of Europe. In the United States, black lesbians and gay men were a vital part of the Harlem Renaissance. This established a pattern that prevailed through much of the century: as social forces brought LGBTQ persons more together and more into the open, reactive cultural and religious factors led to their continued persecution. For example, after World War II members of the U.S. military who were identified as gay were dishonorably discharged and unceremoniously dumped in port towns like San Francisco. Being "outed" in this way typically led to the secondary persecution of gay and bisexual men being ostracized by their families and communities back home. Paradoxically, this worked to solidify the formation of accepting neighborhoods and to the notion of a (somewhat) cohesive LGBTQ community.

The 1950s saw a hardening of a particular view of "traditional family values." This consolidation of a strict portrayal of what counts as "normal" (white, middle class, heterosexual, and Christian) was central to the changing economy, which was increasingly dependent on self-contained nuclear families aspiring to similar patterns of consumption. The consolidation of a rigid view of ideal families was also, in part, a response to the perceived threat to American identity posed by the Cold War. In this context, most behavior that deviated from this narrow (heterosexist) norm was seen not only as simply different but also dangerous. It was construed to be a threat to American strength and unity.

At the same time, groups of support and community for LGBTQ persons formed, not just in neighborhoods but also in particular establishments. The Stonewall Inn in Greenwich Village was just such a place. Here people who were not welcome in their own families, churches, or social circles formed a space of relative safety and a network of support. For many years places like Stonewall were subject to harassment and violence. Such incidents usually went unreported, because to do so was to bring attention that some members of the community shunned. Yet when the police raided Stonewall in 1969, patrons resisted and neighbors rallied. The Stonewall uprising lasted for three days and received wide media attention, beginning a new phase of LGBTQ life in the United States. Influenced by antiwar activists and the Black Power movement, gay activist organizations began to form almost immediately, including the Gay Liberation Front and the Gay Activists Alliance. The first anniversary of the Stonewall riots, June 28, 1970, was marked by Gay Pride marches in Los Angeles and Chicago. During pride marches, LGBTQ people openly celebrated their gender identities and sexual orientations, which both challenged prejudices and fostered community.

While the LGBTQ community made substantial gains during the 1970s, the same decade saw a backlash from conservative Christian groups, bringing renewed energy to heterosexism in the United States. Many ministers and church leaders declared the judgment of God against all forms of same-sex love. A particular way of reading the Bible—a very specific type of interpretation—was used to support this claim. Brief passages of Scripture were plucked out of their historical and literary contexts. Literalist interpretations of those Scriptures were declared to reveal their only possible meaning, with no thought for the Bible's larger message. Thus were LGBTQ persons singled out as under particular divine judgment. This method of interpreting the Bible would have been unrecognizable to many Christians around the world and across the centuries, who believe that the Bible has inexhaustible layers of meaning. It is illuminating that this way of reading Scripture was popularized in America in the context of arguments about slavery. Supporters of slavery picked isolated verses of the Bible that refer to slavery and claimed that these bits of Scripture justified slavery, while abolitionists spoke of the larger meaning of the text in revealing the love of God for all people.[6]

A particularly vital development in the late 1980s was the formation of Gay-Straight Alliances (GSAs). Primarily student led, these are groups formed in middle schools and high schools that have fostered support of LGBTQ people. Often the students attempting to form these groups have met with significant resistance from administrators, parents, and school boards. In several states, including Florida, Utah, and California, disputes over the formation of GSAs have been contested in court, even though the formation of GSAs is protected by the First Amendment and the Federal Equal Access Act.[7]

Nevertheless, GSAs have been effective in educating youth about issues related to sexual orientation, which then decreases bullying and harassment in the school community. Activist Jessica Stewart notes, "especially in the case of LGBTQ issues, young people in schools may be vulnerable or excluded. Allies can have a powerful influence in ending bullying or fostering acceptance." In the 1990s, it was common on college campuses to see pink or rainbow-colored stickers on dorm rooms identifying them as a "safe space" for LBGTQ people. Often hosting Coming Out Day celebrations and other events, GSAs create more accepting communities, boost performance and health of LGBTQ students, and have lasting effects on how young people perceive those who are LGBTQ.

One distinctive aspect of GSAs is their embrace of straight allies. Because a primary goal is to create more acceptance among the whole student population, GSAs are not mainly affinity groups for those who identify as LGBTQ but rather communities designed to include outreach to those who identify as straight. GSAs welcome straight people and provide clear, relatively easy ways to be part of the movement for LGBTQ equality. For example, some GSAs offer buttons with "ally" printed on them. It is easy to affix a button to a backpack. It also has a real effect. More buttons signal that heterosexual behavior is becoming less acceptable in the community. Social and educational events designed to engage straight people are part of the programming of GSAs. A national organization called the GSA Network reports that in some local GSAs, "straight ally youth comprise the majority of a club."[8]

Due to the efforts of LGBTQ activists, many Christian communities and individual Christians now understand the diversity of gender identity and sexual orientation as part of the blessing of God's creation. LGBTQ people are welcomed in many churches. However, many elements of Christianity continue to contribute to heterosexism. The official teaching of the Roman Catholic church—the largest body of Christians in the world—defines same-sex activity as "intrinsically disordered."[9] At the same time, there are many Catholics whose consciences, which are the strongest guide for moral action in Catholic theology, dictate full acceptance of LGBTQ people. There are also many LGBTQ Catholics. Many Protestant denominations aim for full inclusivity and celebrate both same-sex marriage and ordination of LGBTQ people. However, other Protestant church communities remain virulently opposed to same-sex love.

In 2003 the Supreme Court found all antisodomy laws to be unconstitutional (though antisodomy laws remain on the books of several states). Although sexual orientation may not be cause for discrimination in employment by the government, the LGBTQ community has not been definitively declared a protected class of people and is thus subject to discrimination in employment (as well as housing, public accommodations, and credit) in twenty-eight states that do not explicitly include LGBTQ in their anti-discrimination laws.[10] Lesbian, gay, and bisexual people were not allowed to openly serve in the armed forces until 2011. Same-sex marriage was legalized throughout the United States in 2015. However, since then state legislatures have proposed over one hundred bills to allow discrimination of LGBTQ people in employment, service, and housing. Some of these bills would allow doctors to refuse service to LGBTQ people while others would legislate that transgender people have to use the bathroom that matches the sex listed on their birth certificate. The effect of the whole wave of proposed legislation is to fight against the recent gains made by the LGBTQ community in the United States.

While reliable statistics on the extent of anti-LGBTQ violence are difficult to gather (and more difficult to assess over time), attacks on LGBTQ persons have been a persistent and shameful feature of American heterosexism. This is highlighted by the "gay bashing" perpetrated by various police forces in the 1960s, the assassination of Harvey Milk—one of America's first openly gay elected officials—in San Francisco in 1978, the brutal murder of Matthew Shepherd in 1998, and the Orlando massacre of 2016. People of color who are LGBTQ are the targets of hate violence more often than white people who are LGBTQ.[11]

The Role of Allies

Allies have been vital to the movement for LGBTQ liberation, and many white, straight people have found it easier to step into the role of ally with LGBTQ communities than with black communities. Looking closely at some of the factors that have smoothed the way for straight people to be allies in the LGBTQ movement can shed light on being an ally more generally, and on why it can be particularly difficult in antiracist work. One significant difference that has ripple effects for allies is that gender identity and sexual orientation pertain to individuals, while race, especially blackness, is socially constructed as hereditary and therefore pertaining to families.[12]

Welcome

The individual nature of sexual orientation might be one reason that many people in the struggle for LGBTQ equality have been consistently welcoming to straight allies. People who are LGBTQ have not been able to rely on families that share their oppression. Historically, Black people in the United States have found sources of strength and joy in kinship networks and church communities.[13] Individuals who are LGBTQ have often been cast out of such relationships. Creating other forms of community—whether in the closet or out, with LGBTQ people and with straight people—has been necessary for survival. Several LGBTQ organizations, including PFLAG and GSAs, have actively welcomed straight allies and invited them to be part of the struggle.

Relationship

Similarly, because gender identity and sexual orientation pertains to individuals, there are LGBTQ people in nearly everyone's family or close circle of friends. Many people who think that same-sex love is wrong then discover that a person they already know and care for is gay or lesbian. At that moment, two beliefs are in conflict: (1) that same-sex love is perverse and (2) that this beloved individual is LGBTQ and not perverse. The incoherence pressures the person to give up one of these two beliefs. Tragically, many people give up the second belief and reject their friend or family member. Others do not. Many people who find themselves in this moment of conflicted beliefs allow the prior relationship to hold sway. They allow their knowledge of this particular friend or family member to change their minds about same-sex love in general. Consider the early years of PFLAG, when courageous parents who discovered that their children were LGBTQ simply decided to keep loving them. GSA network reports "[s]traight youth are often members of GSAs because they have lesbian, gay, bisexual, or transgender (LGBT) family or friends."[14]

Classism

Because LGBTQ identity pertains to individuals, the economic effects of heterosexism are not necessarily passed on from generation to generation. Many LGBTQ individuals experience oppression that robs them of employment and assets, prevents wealth-building, and causes financial ruin. Of course this has ramifications for the children of people who endure this. Yet the children are not permanently marked with the LGBTQ identity targeted by oppressive structures. Broadly speaking, LGBTQ identity is only loosely entangled with classism.

This makes it possible for middle-class and wealthy straight people to ally with LGBTQ struggles without addressing classism directly. Some activism, focused on helping middle-class straight people understand that LGBTQ people are more similar than they are different, has framed the movement for LGBTQ equality as a struggle for *inclusion* within, and *acceptance* by, the dominant culture in the United States. Various corporations have fostered this after identifying people who are LGBTQ as a market share worth pursuing. Images of gay and lesbian couples that exemplify the middle-class nuclear family, with wedding registries and a new, suburban home, abounded in materials supporting marriage equality. Put bluntly, the LGBTQ struggle has often been promoted and perceived as a white, middle-class movement.

The movement for LGBTQ equality has always been more than this. Full inclusion and acceptance of LGBTQ people holds the promise of radical change toward justice for all of us as it challenges the categories of gender upon which sexism depends. The extravagantly dressed participants in a pride march are not trying to blend in with white suburbia. However, elements of the movement have been organized around concerns of white, middle-class people. This makes it easier for straight people to imagine that the goal is to include LGBTQ persons into social structures that remain unchanged. Furthermore, the various ways in which heterosexism intersects with racism, classism, and other forms of structural oppression are frequently downplayed or neglected.

Each of these factors will be revisited in the practical section of the book. Before we can address them wisely, we need to understand more about racism in the United States.

RACISM

To understand racism in the twenty-first century, we must first look at its origins and development. There is a good deal of U.S. history that is neglected in our textbooks. This history—of slave codes, black codes, segregation, and the criminalization of black life—reveals the roots of division that make it difficult to cross boundaries between white and black Americans today. The discomfort and fear many white people feel about jumping into the struggle for racial equality, as well as the hesitance some black people have regarding white participation, stems from a concrete past. Remembering this past is crucial to changing the future.

Race as a Social Construct: Some Examples from History

Let us look first at the history of the *idea* of race. While people have come in various shades of color for millennia; we were not always classified into races. Race is a socially constructed concept. There was a time and place in which it became expedient to start classifying people based on their physical characteristics, most notably the color of their skin, and to attach meaning to these characteristics. The construction of race in the Western Hemisphere took place in the context of colonial conquest. Before this era, different communities largely defined themselves in terms of family relations, religious practices, languages, and geographical roots. When European colonizers arrived, they often largely did not care to understand the distinctions between tribes, family groups, languages, religious practices, or geographical regions that indigenous peoples used to identify themselves. Instead, the colonizers grouped the various peoples of a continent together, as one mass, which was then named and identified from the colonizers' perspective.

Theologian Willie James Jennings argues that the severing of identity from geography—separating who people are from the land they inhabit—was vital to the social construction of race. Only when large groups of people moved from one place to another—across countries and continents—did it became possible and useful to identify them not primarily on the basis of geographical ties but on the basis of skin color. As people moved (some voluntarily and many forcibly) in large numbers, identity was no longer determined by where a person lived but by what a person looked like—black, white, yellow, or red. Jennings says that without geography to tether identity, "human skin was asked to fly solo and speak for itself."[15]

Skin color became the marker used by European colonizers to classify the different peoples they encountered in their global travels. These categories of race were in a hierarchy from the very beginning. White people always placed themselves at the top by force. Yellow-, brown-, red-, and black-skinned peoples were subjugated and understood to be inferior to whites, an understanding that legitimated the European conquest and enslavement of peoples. It is important to understand that racial categories did not stem from neutral observation of differing skin tones. These categories were created by colonizers to enable and justify the subjugation of other peoples.[16]

This classification system was fragile, at first, and threatened by alliances across racial boundaries.[17] Wealthy European colonizers were outnumbered in the early American colonies by Native Americans, enslaved Africans, and indentured Europeans. In 1676, a plantation owner in Virginia named Nathaniel Bacon gathered enslaved Africans and indentured European immigrants into a coalition based on shared economic interests. This was a class-based, rather than race-based, group. Bacon organized this armed militia and successfully (albeit briefly) overthrew the Virginia colonial government.

In the wake of Bacon's Rebellion, the colonial leaders sought to prevent further threats to their control of the people and land by replacing notions of class solidarity with ones of racial identity. Racial divisions were codified in America as a way for the wealthy to exert social control over the poor. For the first time in the American colonies, the terms "white" and "black" were written into law. With the slave codes, written between 1680 and 1682, "black" became a racial identity that marked who was subject to enslavement. Legal language and public rhetoric moved from describing people as either "slave" or "free" to describing people as "black" or "white."[18]

Shamefully, much of Christian theology was deeply involved with colonial conquest, slavery, and the portrayal of black people as not fully human. Through a series of papal bulls in the fifteenth century, the Roman Catholic Church declared that Christians could claim ownership of lands occupied by non-Christians for European Christian monarchs. This "Doctrine of Discovery" declared that inhabitants of such lands should be converted; those who refused could be enslaved or killed. This theology influenced a series of later decisions by the United States Supreme Court in the early nineteenth century. These rulings supported colonizers' claim to lands they had "discovered" during the previous three centuries.

During the eighteenth and nineteenth centuries many

Christians argued that slavery was divinely ordained. Josiah Priest published a popular book titled *Bible Defence of Slavery; or the Origin, History, and Fortunes of the Negro Race.*[19] George Whitefield, an evangelist who was influential in the Great Awakening in the eighteenth century, found the conditions of slavery abhorrent when he first came to the American colonies. Whitefield preached to black and white people together. However, after spending more time in Georgia, Whitefield became accustomed enough to slavery to advocate its expansion.[20] While several Christian denominations split over the issue of slavery, only one sect—the Religious Society of Friends, or Quakers—completely rejected slavery before 1776.

Because slavery in the United States was justified through the social construction of black people as an inferior race, when slavery was officially outlawed its ideology was not repudiated. White supremacy had simply become too deeply entrenched in public policy and popular imagination for the end of slavery to substantially alter it.

Political freedom was promised to black Americans in the Civil Rights Act of 1866. The Civil Rights Act granted citizenship and the same rights enjoyed by white citizens to all *male* persons in the United States, *"without distinction of race or color, or previous condition of slavery or involuntary servitude."* The goal of increasing liberty and opportunity for black Americans was taken up by significant governmental forces and supported throughout the South by federal troops and Freedmen's Bureau's during a period of time referred to as Reconstruction. For a brief moment, black men participated in the political process and were elected to state and federal office. During the 1870s, over two thousand black men were elected to office, including sixteen to Congress.[21] Just ten years later, however, the progress of Reconstruction was bartered away by white politicians in a disputed presidential election. In 1876, Democrats conceded the White House to Republican Rutherford Hayes in return for an end to Reconstruction.[22]

Federal troops were withdrawn from the South, Freedmen's Bureaus were closed, and a new series of laws that effectively re-enslaved thousands of African Americans were enacted. These "black codes" were enacted to replace the "slave codes" of the previous era. These laws included:

- prohibitions on vagrancy—that is, one had to prove they were employed or be subject to arrest,
- prohibitions on learning how to read and write,
- prohibitions on assembling without a white person present,
- prohibitions on being intoxicated,
- prohibitions on living in white communities,
- prohibitions on marrying whites, and
- prohibitions on servants leaving their employers' home without permission and numerous laws prescribing segregation of the races.[23]

Black people convicted of violating these laws could be whipped, branded, or imprisoned. Many of the black men convicted of these "offenses" never went to prison because their sentences were sold to the owners of coal mines, brick factories, and businesses such as the U.S. Steel Corporation. This new system of slavery became a significant source of revenue for several southern states while providing a cheap source of labor to industry. This continued into the 1940s.[24]

The brief period of Reconstruction in the 1870s proved that if black people are able to vote, they can effectively participate in the political process. Soon after Reconstruction ended, various laws were enacted to limit black access to the ballot box, including: literacy tests, poll taxes, outright violence, the loss of voting rights due to felony convictions, and voter ID laws. All were attempts to limit black access to the ballot box and thus to political power.[25]

The abandonment of Reconstruction after the contested election of 1876, the "black codes" that placed intolerable restrictions on the rights of black citizens, Jim Crow laws and the disenfranchisement of black voters—all pointed to the fact that U.S. laws and social structures defined what was good for (white) America in terms of what was bad for black Americans.

Nothing demonstrates this reality more clearly than the lynchings of the late nineteenth and early twentieth centuries. Between 1877 and 1950 roughly four thousand black men, women, and children were lynched.[26] The "reasons" for the extrajudicial torture and murder of black people could be anything that was perceived as threatening the white superiority in governing, industry, and social life or the "honor" of white women. Lynchings were not acts of vigilante justice but rather a brutal method of intimidation and social control of black Americans. The white people who participated in lynchings were not indicted or convicted of crimes. To the contrary, sometimes lynchings were advertised in the local paper ahead of time. They were typically public events attended by crowds of white people who packed a picnic lunch to enjoy with their family while witnessing the dangling body of a fellow human being. People wore their best church clothes and posed for photographs in front of their victim.[27] Some spectator/participants purchased bits of the corpse as souvenirs.[28] The point of these lynchings was to demonstrate to the entire country that white people could still kill black people with impunity and to remind black people that their own lives could be taken at any moment with no reason or justice.[29]

At the same time, there were many attempts to establish "scientific" delineations for racial distinctions based on blood or head shape. These went hand in hand with efforts to "scientifically" demonstrate the superiority of white people. The assumptions and methods of these studies were wildly unscientific. There continues to be no scientific basis for racial distinctions, even though as recently as 1923 the U.S. Supreme Court was issuing rulings about who is and is not white.[30] The infamous "one-drop rule," which declared a person to be black if they have one drop of "black blood," was not passed into law in the United States until the 1924 Racial Integrity Act. Two people who looked exactly alike could be legally determined to be of different races based on the notion that one had a far-distant relative from sub-Saharan Africa. This rule was created to reinforce white supremacy in the Jim Crow South. Both white supremacy and the importance of the black/white divide in the history of the United States have had wide-ranging effects on people of other ethnic identities. When the one-drop rule was passed in Virginia, every person in the state was deemed either white or black, including people who were Native Americans.

This history emphasizes that racial categories have never been separated from their original context and purpose—colonial conquest and slavery. Race is always bound up to the larger system of white supremacy that created it. This means "white" and "black" have never been parallel categories. One drop of "black blood" rendered a person "black," while one drop of "white blood" did not render a person "white." Whiteness was equated with a purity that could be defiled by blackness.

Furthermore, these racial categories cannot be untangled from issues of class. The same legislation (the slave codes) that defined blackness as a liability—to be black was to be property— defined whiteness as a financial asset.[31] White people could not be enslaved, could own property, had greater access to education and employment, and so forth. The economic benefits of whiteness continued through public policies enacted throughout the twentieth century.

The New Deal refers to a group of economic programs implemented in the 1930s to aid recovery from the Great Depression. While it offered significant financial assistance to white people, several of the programs excluded black people.

One of the New Deal programs, Social Security, is the most successful antipoverty program in U.S. history. When the Social Security Act was passed in 1935, it explicitly excluded agricultural and domestic workers as well as government employees, self-employed persons, and a few other groups. Excluding agricultural and domestic workers meant that 65 percent of employed black persons were ineligible for Social Security benefits.[32]

The Federal Housing Administration (FHA), created in 1934, has been the most effective wealth building initiative in our history for the middle and working classes. Prior to the FHA, typical terms for buying a home included a 50 percent down payment and a five-year mortgage. Very few Americans could afford to purchase a home. The Roosevelt administration changed the terms of home ownership by backing mortgages made by the banks. This lowered down payment requirements to 20 percent of the asking price or less, and it extended the term for a mortgage up to thirty years. Suddenly, monthly mortgage payments became as affordable as monthly rent payments. However, the FHA only guaranteed mortgages in neighborhoods deemed to be safe bets for lending. Given the realities of racism, this translated into color-coded maps for every neighborhood in the nation in which neighborhoods that had been "infiltrated" by people who were Jewish or black were colored in red and deemed "hazardous" for lending. This practice, called redlining,[33] enforced segregation and offered an enormous wealth building opportunity to whites alone. Between 1934 and 1962 the federal government guaranteed $120 billion of FHA mortgages, propelling millions of Americans into home ownership and the middle class. 98 percent of those mortgages went to white Americans.

The pattern of inequality in the New Deal was repeated with the Servicemen's Readjustment Act of 1944. Commonly called the G.I. Bill, this provided low cost mortgages, financial assistance for education, and a series of other benefits for veterans. The G.I. Bill did not explicitly exclude black people, but it was administered in such a way that discrimination on a local level was pervasive. One historian states that the effects of the G.I. Bill were "more racially distinct and arguably more cruel than any other New Deal-era program."[34]

In the 1970s, the government's drug policy gave new form to these prior methods of social control in service of white supremacy. The phrase "war on drugs" came into use after President Richard Nixon declared drugs "public enemy number one" in 1971. Imagining that the United States is involved in a war on drugs has helped convince American citizens and elected officials to allow billions of dollars to be spent in military aid and intervention in multiple countries as well as to enact harsh sentencing laws within the United States. This failed drug policy has done massive harm at home and abroad, and it has disproportionately hurt black and brown people.[35]

John Ehrlichman, a member of the Nixon Administration who was convicted of conspiracy after Watergate, describes the origins of the War on Drugs as explicitly racial:

> The Nixon campaign in 1968, and the Nixon White House after that, had two enemies: the antiwar left and black people. You understand what I'm saying? We knew we couldn't make it illegal to be either against the war or black, but by getting the public to associate the hippies with marijuana and blacks with heroin, and then criminalizing both heavily, we could disrupt those communities. We could arrest their leaders, raid their homes, break up their meetings, and vilify them night after night on the evening news. Did we know we were lying about the drugs? Of course we did.[36]

Black Life in the Contemporary United States

On August 9, 2014, a police officer named Darren Wilson stopped an unarmed black teenager named Michael Brown in Ferguson, Missouri, reportedly for the crime of jaywalking. During an interaction that lasted only ninety seconds, Wilson shot and killed Brown. After the killing, Michael Brown's body was left, uncovered, in the August heat, for four hours and thirty-two minutes. His corpse was on display in front of neighbors, family, friends, and children. For many—probably most—white people, those four hours and thirty-two minutes are among the lesser details of this unfortunate story. For most black people, they are a chilling echo of the lynchings that terrorized their community—and a reminder of what has and has not changed in the years since.

One thing that has not changed can be called the "criminalization of black life." After middle class residents and employment opportunities moved farther out from city centers in the mid to late twentieth century, some financially struggling municipalities turned to fines to balance their budgets. Fines for parking infractions, traffic violations, and even "tall grass" were levied on residents so that the city could pay its bills. Given the demographics of these municipalities, this meant targeting poor people and black people. When the Department of Justice investigated policing in Ferguson, they found rampant exploitation of the population for economic gain. Section III of the DOJ report is titled "Ferguson Law Enforcement Efforts are Focused on Generating Revenue;" Section IV is titled "Ferguson Law Enforcement Practices Violate the Law and Undermine Community Trust, Especially Among African Americans."[37] The "key findings" of the Ferguson report are particularly disturbing; here are a few:

- The 67% of African Americans in Ferguson account for 93% of arrests made from 2012–2014.
- A Ferguson woman parked her car illegally once in 2007. It ended up costing her more than $1,000 and six days in jail.
- The disproportionate number of arrests, tickets, and use of force stemmed from "unlawful bias" rather than black people committing more crime.
- A singled missed, late, or partial payment of a fine could mean jail time.
- Arrest warrants are "almost exclusively" used as threats to push for payments.[38]

White and black Americans use drugs at roughly the same rates. However, black people are much more likely to be arrested for drug related charges.[39] One of the factors in the higher arrest rates of African Americans is home ownership. Since white people are more likely to live in a private home, drug use often takes place in the relative safety and privacy of their home or a friend's home. Since black people are more likely to rent, their drug use often takes place in a park or an apartment building. When this living situation is combined with the elevated levels of policing and the preponderance of closed circuit surveillance cameras on utility poles, ATM machines, and bodegas, black people are more susceptible to being caught. The higher population density of apartment-filled areas, as opposed to suburbs, means that apartment dwellers are also more likely to live in a "Drug Free School Zone" where sentencing is harsher.[40]

Aspects of the war on drugs have had even more explicit racial bias. Crack and powdered cocaine are the same drug. The difference is that crack can be purchased in smaller quantities than powdered cocaine, making crack more accessible to poor people. Since black people are disproportionately poor, the use of crack has been higher among black people, while white people more often use powdered cocaine.[41] In 1986, congress passed the Anti-Drug Abuse Act of 1986, which equated possession of five grams (about five raisins) of crack cocaine with possession of five hundred grams of powdered cocaine. This meant that black people faced much longer sentences for having the same quantities of the same drug as white people. The explicit racial bias of this law was challenged, and in 2010 the 100:1 disparity was reduced to 18:1.

Another aspect of the same story is the emergence of "stop and frisk" and "broken windows" policing strategies. Sold to the public as an antigang procedure and a way to keep property values high, these practices amount to a new form of black codes.[42] Municipalities pass local injunctions like curfews, antiloitering rules, and antiassociation laws that encourage police officers to stop, question, and frisk people on the street. Sometimes these policies were explicitly linked to practices of racial profiling, meaning officers and security guards were instructed to stop black and brown people, especially men. In other circumstances "stop and frisk" or "broken windows" policing policies were not overtly tied to race but were almost exclusively employed in areas with high population density—that is, neighborhoods with apartments instead of single-family homes.

Given the close ties between race, homeownership, and wealth, these policies effectively criminalized urban black life. White teenage boys can play ball in the yard of their house without fear of being frisked by the police and questioned for trespassing or loitering. Black teenage boys attempting to play the same ballgame often do so in spaces deemed public, such as the hallway or front stoop of the apartment building they live in, where antiloitering and antiassociation laws are in place. A sign with letters stenciled in spray paint hangs on the front door of an apartment building in a black neighborhood. It reads: "No Loitering, No Trespassing, Police Take Notice TENANTS INCLUDED." A ballgame on a summer evening thus becomes a criminal activity.

After the death of Freddie Gray, allegations of misconduct sparked a Department of Justice (DOJ) investigation of the Baltimore Police Department. The DOJ report, released in 2016, included forms for officers to fill out whenever they stopped someone. These forms had blank spaces for the name of the person stopped, the time and place, and so forth. However, templates for arrest warrants for trespass had certain fields already filled in, namely the race and sex of the suspect: "Black male."[43]

Imagine a young white man with a small amount of marijuana. If he lives in the suburbs, he will likely go unnoticed. Imagine by contrast, a young black man in the city sitting on the front stoop of his own apartment. He is approached by police officers who charge him with loitering or trespassing. When they search him, they find a small amount of marijuana. Since the apartment is in a Drug Free School Zone, the young man now has three charges: trespass, possession of marijuana, and violating a Drug Free School Zone.

If our imaginary white suburbanite was arrested for possession (a single charge), he might well be able to afford a private attorney. Our imaginary black urbanite is assigned an overworked public defender who quickly reviews his case and suggests a plea bargain. The prosecutor offers to drop the trespass charge if the young man pleads guilty to the other two. According to the Justice Department upwards of 95 percent of all court appearances end in a plea bargain rather than a trial![44] Furthermore, research pertaining to Manhattan (and perhaps indicative of practices elsewhere) has shown that black people aren't offered plea bargains as advantageous as those offered to white defendants:

- Black defendants were 19 percent more likely than whites to be offered plea deals that included jail or prison time.
- Blacks and Latinos charged with misdemeanor person offenses or drug offenses were more likely to be held in jail or prison at their arraignment.
- Blacks and Latinos were both significantly more likely to be offered plea deals that included time behind bars for misdemeanor drug offenses. For misdemeanor marijuana cases in particular, blacks were 19 percent more likely to be offered a plea deal that required time behind bars.[45]

A criminal conviction, particularly a drug conviction, is interpreted by many as a mark of immorality. More concretely, it makes legal all manner of discrimination. Most job applications inquire about an applicant's criminal past.[46] A felony drug conviction makes one ineligible for college financial aid and makes way for legal discrimination in employment and housing. A convicted felon can be denied the right to serve on a jury, the right to receive public assistance, and even the right to vote. Nationally, 5.85 million Americans and one out of every thirteen African

Americans have lost the right to vote. The disenfranchisement of those convicted of felonies affects black Americans at a rate four times greater than the rest of America, replicating the effects of poll taxes and literacy tests of the Jim Crow era.[47]

America remains a highly racially (and economically) segregated society. This segregation can take the form of visible, physical barriers. In Detroit there is the "8 Mile Wall,"[48] a six feet high, one foot thick, half mile long concrete wall built in 1941 so that a new white community could be built with FHA loans because it was walled off from the surrounding black neighborhood. A more pervasive use of the built environment to racially segregate our society has been the placement of rail lines[49] and interstate highways.[50] At the same time, segregation relies not only on visible barriers but also on other structural means of separation.

White and black Americans may work together in increasing numbers, but we continue to live, study, dine, play, vacation, worship, and love in two separate, different, and unequal Americas. For decades this segregation was legally prescribed. When people attempted to dismantle the oppression of this segregation, their plight was denied. The 1896 court decision Plessy v. Ferguson enshrined the ideal of "separate but equal" into American law. That ruling was struck down in 1954 by the Brown v. Board of Education Supreme Court decision, which stated clearly that, "separate educational facilities are inherently unequal." In *Brown* the Court wrote,"Does segregation of children in public schools solely on the basis of race, even though the physical facilities and other tangible factors may be equal, deprive the children of the minority group of equal educational opportunities? We believe that it does."[51]

While the doctrine of "separate but equal" is no longer the law of the land, we still have not learned the lesson of *Brown*. It appears that most white Americans either disagree with the premise that segregation is tantamount to inequality, or we have deemed this inequality acceptable.

Simply put, white and black Americans don't know each other, don't understand each other, and don't trust each other. As argued previously, racism is structural and systemic, and it helps to perpetuate racism when we keep our focus on individuals and attitudes. At the same time, we must acknowledge that we are shaped and formed by the structures in which we live, such that systemic racism infiltrates our perception and interpretation of the world around us. It is not possible to live in a society where the prevailing discourse on race for four hundred years has been to demonize, infantilize, pathologize, and criminalize black lives without internalizing at least some of that thinking. We have imbibed negative images of black people through film, television, music, literature, the law, the news media, and countless other sources. This influences us on a subconscious level, developing what social scientists refer to as implicit bias. This means that a person who may never entertain an explicitly racist thought can still be more likely to associate being black with being criminal or being white with being trustworthy.

Often white people in the United States are so segregated from black people—and live such separate lives—that the stereotypes that surround us have no counter in our own experiences. This leads to profoundly prejudiced and bigoted views being commonplace and unremarkable within white communities.

For instance, a white clerk and a recently retired white New Yorker customer had the following exchange in rural, white Connecticut:

> **Customer:** "I came to this area to get away from these people."
>
> **Clerk:** "By themselves they're not bad."
>
> **Customer:** "Yeah, but where you have one you have the family, and then you have the drugs. . . ."
>
> **Clerk:** "Yeah, we do have an infestation of them. . . ."

The clerk knew a couple black customers, but absent any meaningful relationships, he carried on with this racist dialogue publicly.

Because this exchange continued when another person, a white person, entered the one-room store, it is clear that the men felt comfortable in their discourse—a reflection that the standards of their community accept a level of racist speaking that may not be more widely accepted.

Separation and segregation are the lifeblood of racism. White people who aspire to be allies must cross the boundaries that divide us and seek out mutual relationships with African Americans. This does not mean that the ultimate goal of allyship is having more black friends. Because racism is structural and systematic, it cannot be undone without significant changes in policy, law, and concrete practices. Yet these structural changes will not happen while segregation and separation enable implicit bias and rampant ignorance to flourish.

This brief history lesson does not begin to touch on the full picture of the unfolding of racism in the United States. It does not address all of the policy decisions and legislation that have made life easier for white people and harder for black people. It does not address all of the ways in which current events are interpreted differently by white and black people due to how little of this history white people know. Much more could be said in regard to sexuality, sports, nutrition, medical care, education, the arts, and more. In each of these areas, historical events driven by white supremacy have shaped structures that continue to influence our common life.

Allies

Over the course of American history, there have been white people who allied themselves with black people struggling against racism. However, those of us who want to be allies can find it difficult to know how to begin. There are a number of specific reasons for this.

Welcome

White people often do not know if their presence or work in the struggle is desired. This has historical roots. Martin Luther King Jr. encouraged white people to be involved and invited people of all faiths to join in the civil rights movement by participating in concrete actions. Only a small minority of white people responded, and some of those who did behaved badly. They were paternalistic in their attitudes and actions, and they did not face the same dangers and consequences as black activists. The black power movement brought awareness to, and disapproval of, these patterns.[52] In 1967 the Student Nonviolent Coordinating Committee, one of the most influential groups challenging white supremacy, asked its white members to leave the group.[53] After welcoming white people into the struggle, there was such paternalism that black activists felt they needed to rescind the invitation.

Today, there are many invitations being issued to white people to participate in concrete actions for racial justice. Several prominent activists, such as Rev. Dr. William Barber II, and organizations, such as PICO National Network, actively welcome white people into the struggle. There are also organizations, such as Standing Up for Racial Justice (SURJ), that focus explicitly on the work white people can do. However, the segregation of white and black Americans means that many white people are completely unaware that such invitations have been made.

Relationship

The history of geographic and social segregation of white and black people in the United States means that many white people are not in personal relationships with black people. The kind of prior relationship that could make a person rethink their prejudice against LGBTQ people often does not exist across racial lines. For a white person who does not have personal relationships with black people, the prejudice and bias that are promulgated in various forms of media go unchecked by personal experience. The pain of black communities over the killing of unarmed black men, black women, and black children by police officers can be a distant reality to a white person in our segregated country. And the stories of injustice can seem unbelievable to a population that has not experienced them firsthand. For white people whose hearts are broken by news reports, it can be hard to find a way to join in the work for justice if there are no black people in your neighborhood, town, or county.

Classism
One factor that contributes to geographic segregation is the absence of inherited wealth (such as home equity) in many black families. There are also large differences in the financial fortunes of white and black communities overall. While many black people have achieved financial success, in broad terms white people have more money. The wealth gap between white and black people has been created by the history summarized in this chapter; it was systematically generated by the slave codes, the black codes, New Deal policies, and the criminalization of black life.

However, as mentioned earlier, it can be difficult for Americans to perceive these structures and their consequences because we value a sense of rugged individualism and personal responsibility. This combination fuels the structural oppression of classism and enables middle class and wealthy people to believe that those who are less affluent are so by their own choice or failing.

Every white person who desires to be an ally for black liberation faces the obstacle of classism. For middle class and wealthy white people, this can mean confronting their own prejudice against poor people. Also, it challenges a person's sense of self to recognize that his or her success is not entirely due to hard work but also due to the unearned advantages of being white in a racist system.

For poor white people, being at an antiracist ally can pose a different set of challenges. Descriptions of white privilege can be very hard to take for white people who are barely scraping by economically. Yet an even more important difficulty is revealed in the history discussed above. Racial segregation was written into Virginia law by wealthy elites to prevent poor Africans and Europeans from banding together following Bacon's Rebellion. Those in power stoked division in order to secure their own status. The same pattern plays out in contemporary politics, as some with wealth and power persuade poor white people that their problems are not caused by policies that benefit the very rich but rather by people of color, be they immigrants or African Americans. Furthermore, throughout the history of the United States, whiteness has been a financial asset.[54] Racial justice would devalue the currency of whiteness, and would therefore take a financial asset away from white people. For poor white people who have few assets to begin with, this can appear threatening.

The added obstacles of classism do not mean that white people—poor, middle class, or wealthy—cannot become allies in the struggle for racial justice. But it does add another layer of complication and difficulty to the task.

These three factors—welcome, relationship, and classism—function very differently in efforts to become an ally for LGBTQ equality and for racial justice. In regard to each of these factors, it is a bit easier to be an ally to the LGBTQ community. We believe these differences are influenced by—and perhaps rooted in—the reality that gender identity and sexual orientation pertain to individuals while race is socially constructed as pertaining to families. In addition, there is a fourth factor that complicates the task of being an antiracist ally: white guilt.

Guilt

In extremely general terms, straight people are less likely to be overwhelmed with a sense of guilt when we become more aware of heterosexism than white people are when we become more aware of racism. Understanding that we, as heterosexuals, garner unearned benefits from unjust social structures does not immediately translate into guilt and self-defense.

We suspect that the issue of guilt is also affected by the fact that gender orientation and sexual identity are in two ways characteristics of individuals rather than families. First, often when we realize that LGBTQ people have been oppressed, and even that we have been part of such oppression, we are dealing with individuals. Instead of facing the entire weight of corporate racism, we can sometimes face the reality that our friend or sister or nephew is hurting. Sometimes we realize apologies are due to friends or family members, but these are personal relationships in which apologies are possible. Second, for cisgender heterosexuals, our sexual identity is also experienced as an individual characteristic. We do not feel a kinship with all straight people to such a degree that we feel that heterosexuals who create and sustain oppressive structures are "our people."

Intersectionality

In the intersection between racism and heterosexism, LGBTQ people of color are doubly oppressed. Sometimes their concerns and leadership are also not brought to the forefront of the struggle itself. Likewise, some black communities, including churches, have been slow to support LGBTQ liberation. While one would hope that people who are oppressed in different ways would make common cause with one another, often larger structures promote division.

However, there have been powerful moments of intersectional activism. Many of the participants in the Stonewall riots were people of color. In 1970, Huey P. Newton, cofounder of the Black Panther party, issued a powerful statement that reflected the intersectionality of racism, sexism, and heterosexism long before the term "intersectionality" was coined. He acknowledged the harm done to LGBTQ people, writing, "homosexuals are not given freedom and liberty by anyone in the society. They might be the most oppressed people in the society." He recognized that heterosexism and sexism are related, writing of, "the long conditioning process which builds insecurity in the American male." With extreme candor, Newton wrote, "We want to hit a homosexual in the mouth because we are afraid that we might be homosexual; and we want to hit the women or shut her up because we are afraid that she might castrate us, or take the nuts that we might not have to start with." Newton argued, "We must gain security in ourselves and therefore have respect and feelings for all oppressed people." He said clearly, "the women's liberation front and gay liberation front are our friends, they are our potential allies, and we need as many allies as possible."[55] Today, there are many black LGBTQ activists at the forefront of the Black Lives Matter movement.

In this chapter, we have identified a number of factors that make becoming an ally in the struggle for justice difficult, including issues of welcome, relationship, classism, and guilt. Strategies for addressing these issues will be discussed in the next two sections of this book.

DISCUSSION QUESTIONS

1. How have ways of thinking and talking about LGBTQ issues changed since you were younger? How has your own thinking changed around these issues? What further changes would you like to see?

2. In what ways does your faith shape your thinking about LGBTQ issues? Have you ever experienced tension between your faith and your attitudes toward LGBTQ persons? If so, how have you dealt with that tension?

3. Was the history in this chapter familiar to you? Did you learn about Bacon's Rebellion or redlining in school? At home?

4. In the place where you grew up, were there laws, rules, regulations, or unwritten expectations that placed black persons at an economic or social disadvantage? How aware of these structures were you at the time?

5. The authors emphasize that our society is still very racially segregated. Do a rough assessment of the level of segregation in your own life. Look at your family, your social circles, your neighborhood, your children's classrooms, your bookshelves, your Facebook friends, and your coworkers. How often do you spend time with people of different racial backgrounds?

6. Do you think it has been harder for white people to function as allies in the struggle against racism than it has for straight, cisgender persons to be allies in the struggle for marriage equality and other LGBTQ rights? Have you found this to be the case in your own experience?

CHAPTER TWO

Getting Ready to Be an Ally

Learning more about racism generates a lot of emotions—often painful and conflicting. In the cultural context of the United States, when something has gone wrong, we often move quickly to sort people into the innocent and the guilty. When we begin to recognize the harms of racism and heterosexism, we attempt to apply the same categories. Who is innocent? Who is guilty? However, these categories are not helpful in addressing the complexities of structural oppression. They are too individualistic as well as too simplistic. In order to respond to the call of justice, we need a different framework—one that accounts for both individual and corporate wrongdoing and for the complexity of benefiting from injustice even while fighting it. Christian teaching can provide a more nuanced framework in which to understand injustice and work against it. This is the framework of grace and sin.

INNOCENCE AND GUILT

Our contemporary categories of innocence and guilt are grounded in ideas of individual morality and freedom. We tend to think that we are morally responsible for our individual choices, which makes us either innocent or guilty. Although this seems like common sense to many of us in the United States, it is worth looking closely at the elements and implications of this view.

1. If a person does not choose something, she cannot be held culpable for it. For example, we find it repulsive to read of other cultures where a woman can be punished because she was raped. She did not commit crime; a crime was committed against her!
2. Free choice can only happen when there are options. Even if someone acts of his own accord, without being coerced, we tend to think his freedom is compromised if there were not alternatives to choose from. This is why we can say, "he had no choice."
3. We are each responsible for our own actions. If one person steals money, payment ought not be demanded from another. It would be bizarre to punish one person for the crimes of another.
4. This focus on the freedom of the individual to choose among options means that we think more about particular acts than long-term character. We focus on dramatic choices as the moment of freedom rather than the years of small acts that form a person to be kind and caring, or not to be.[1]

This view of right and wrong is common sense to many people in the United States today, in part because it aligns nicely with capitalism. Freedom as the individual's choice among options is precisely the kind of freedom needed to purchase cereal in aisle seven at the grocery store. It is the kind of freedom needed to "reinvent" oneself with a makeover and a new wardrobe. Every advertising agency in the United States works feverishly to convince us, every day, that our true freedom lies in choosing among options, individually, and always with a sense that we can choose something new tomorrow.

Because this framework of innocence and guilt is so deeply woven into our collective imagination, when people in dominant cultures (white people and straight, cisgender people) learn about the oppression of others in our society, we often move quickly to sort this reality—and ourselves—into the categories of innocence or guilt.

One way to maintain our own innocence is denial. This can take the form of inattention to the plight of others, of skepticism about claims of oppression, or of revisionist history that glosses over the integral role of systemic injustice in the economic, social, legal, and material foundations of the United States.

While denial is understandable in response to hearing about systemic injustice, it is not acceptable. After an initial moment of incredulity—of hope, perhaps, that things cannot be so bad— we must actually do the work of learning and listening. With an abundance of information readily available to substantiate claims of racism and heterosexism, continued denial is a form of willful ignorance and self-deception. It allows structural injustice to thrive, and it does harm to people of color and LGBTQ persons. Every act of denial—every time we do not listen or believe the witness of those who experience oppression—actively contributes to racism and heterosexism. It trades the well-being of other people for a false sense of our own innocence (and the rest of white, heterosexual, cisgender America).

Sometimes denial moves into a grudging acceptance that racism and heterosexism do exist, "*but.* . . ." This "but" can be followed by a number of things intended to show that these forms of oppression should not be taken too seriously. For example, some say that racism and heterosexism are real, *but* they are largely a thing of the past. Another form of the "yes, *but*" response is a counterclaim of oppression. This looks like a woman dismissing accounts of racism by saying she has experienced sexism. Racism is real, she implies, but sexism is worse. While talking about two different forms of oppression can be fruitful, arranging them as opposites that cancel each other out is not. Various forms of oppression do not compete; they compound.

Another strategy for maintaining innocence is to rely on individual intention as the true measure. White people explain that they do not believe that people of color are inferior. Straight people say they have no problem with homosexuality, bisexuality, or transgenderism. Often people state that they were raised to believe that everybody is equal and to treat everybody the same. Such statements can be entirely accurate and yet miss the point completely. They fail to account for the systemic and structural nature of oppression. To return to an earlier analogy, declaring one's love for bicycles does not change the reality that the city is built for cars. Given that racism and heterosexism are baked into the social and economic structures of the United States, we cannot live in this country without participating in these systems. Those of us in the dominant demographics—straight or white people—reap benefits from these systems even if we do not agree with them. Furthermore, our benefits are not merely coincidental with oppression. White people have certain advantages because of the systemic oppression of people of color. We are involved in something that harms other people.

To make matters worse, we cannot cease to reap the benefits of racism and heterosexism. Imagine learning that an ancestor—Mr. White—earned millions through shady business deals. When the executors of the White Smith family estate arrive with your inheritance, a principled response would be to reject the money or find a way to restore it to those who were wronged. However, in the case of systemic oppression, we cannot reject the benefits. Even if we change our names and move to another town, everyone still recognizes us as Mr. White's great-grandchildren. There is a family resemblance. In a million subtle ways, the executors of Grandpa's estate keep tracking us down to deliver another dividend on our inheritance. No matter what we do, or how difficult our lives are, we still receive a little more respect on the subway, a second look in the application pile, a bit more safety, opportunity, authority, and wealth.

If we see the world through the categories of innocence and guilt, then when we realize we cannot escape the systems of oppression that benefit us—we cannot be truly innocent—guilt appears to be our lot. Within our common framework of innocence and guilt, which is fueled in our collective imagination by the ideal (not the actuality) of an impartial justice system, the innocent go free and the guilty are held responsible. If we try to reckon with an understanding of systemic injustice within this framework of innocence and guilt, then the scope of responsibility begins to expand. We are not just responsible for actions we take and options we choose but also for systems from which we benefit.

If we follow this line of reasoning, then white citizens of the United States are responsible for the atrocities of slavery and the ongoing harm of white supremacy and racism. We are responsible for the genocide of Native Americans and the theft of land. We are responsible for the crimes of our peoples in the past, for the harms done to others by white people today, and for the situation into which future generations will be born. Those of us who are straight and cisgender are responsible for the denigration of LGBTQ persons, past and present. We are responsible for the children bullied in school, the teens beaten or kicked out of their homes, the young and older ones who commit suicide. In a globalized world, the politicians we elect and the corporations from which we purchase goods are deeply involved in events around the world that cause harm, so our responsibility knows no geographic limits.

This responsibility, extending through past, present, and future across the entire globe, is more than any person, community, or generation can bear. Taking on the burden of this responsibility, so defined, is not just impractical; it is also based on an untenable conceptual foundation. Our common framework of innocence and guilt is based on evaluating individual, free, moral actions. However, structural oppression is much more than individual actions. Once we start to think about brokenness and inequality in structural and communal ways, our common use of the term "responsibility"—as well as the framework of innocence and guilt—begins to break down.

Christian teaching offers another framework—grace and sin—that is far better suited to the complexities of structural oppression. For anyone interested in working for justice, this aspect of Christian theology can be a helpful tool. Dr. Ludger Viefhues-Bailey, a scholar and college administrator who engages the movements for LGBTQ rights and racial equality, reflects, "the complex problem of responsibility that institutionalized racism and heterosexism produces may require a religious response along the lines of a theology of grace."

GRACE AND SIN

Grace is defined by the *where* and *why* of its origin. Grace comes from God. This origin says something of the content of grace, because as Christians we know something about God, particularly in Jesus Christ, through Scripture, and with the help of the Holy Spirit. The Bible witnesses to God's profound creativity and love. It makes sense, then, that grace, which comes from God, will share these characteristics of creativity and love. We should be extremely hesitant to name anything that is wantonly destructive or hateful as grace. While God has created a world in which destruction and hate are possibilities that do come to pass, these are not grace.

The why of grace is God's own freedom. Grace is given out of God's good pleasure. It cannot be earned, merited, bargained for, or extorted. There is nothing humanity can do to deserve grace, for grace is—by definition—freely given by God.

Three primary forms of grace are creation, salvation, and calling. Our existence is a gift of grace, for God freely created the cosmos. By grace, each and every one of us is a beloved child of God. Christians affirm that we are saved by grace in Jesus Christ—a form of grace that can be understood in myriad ways. Finally, we are called by grace into loving relationship with God and one another.

This calling is offered individually and communally. Loving relationship between God and creation is God's big picture project. We call it the new creation, the kingdom of God, and beatific vision. As Christians, we know that God will make good on this project, that its completion and success are sealed in the resurrection of Jesus Christ. We trust that this future has already begun and will become fully present. This vision is central to Christian life because it shapes our way forward in the world. We attempt to live into this vision, to live here and now in ways that reflect this eternal love of God.

How do we know what this future that God intends for us looks like? We look back, to Scripture and, particularly, to the life and ministry of Jesus Christ. Theologian Letty Russell writes, "Jesus is a memory of the future."[2] Looking back to the ministry of Jesus, we see the character of the future to which we are called by God. This memory helps us to behave now in ways that move us in the direction of this new creation. All of us are invited to get in on the action of what God is doing in the world. We are called to be part of what God is up to by embodying the new creation here and now.

God's large-scale project involves all creation, but it also involves people as individuals. God calls each one of us toward love of God and neighbor, in a way that is personal, individual, and intimate. God's call on our lives is always communal; it is about right relationships, meaning that we can never live into this call alone. At the same time it is personal to each human being. God calls us each by name.

This is the context—the vast narrative of God's loving freedom—in which Christian life unfolds. It is within this context of grace that we speak of sin.

The mention of sin bothers many of us, often for very good reasons. Sin language has been used to condemn and harm many. This is a profound misuse of the doctrine. However, if we approach this doctrine differently, it helps make sense of our lives and holds real promise for our current circumstances. For those of us who aspire to be allies in struggles for justice, sin can be a key category in understanding oppression and how to work against it.

One of the many Greek words translated as "sin" in the Bible means "missing the mark." The most commonly used Hebrew word for sin in the Bible means "to go astray." Sin signals that something is not as it should be. Furthermore, it is a decidedly theological term, in that it has to do with our relationship with God. Throughout the Bible, humanity's relationship with God can never be separated from our relationships with one another. The Gospel of Matthew tells a story in which Jesus is asked,

> "Teacher, which commandment in the law is the greatest?" He said to him, "'You shall love the Lord your God with all your heart, and with all your soul, and with all your mind.' This is the greatest and first commandment. And a second is like it: 'You shall love your neighbor as yourself.' On these two commandments hang all the law and the prophets" (Matt. 22:36–40).

In the Gospel of Luke, this is presented not as two commandments but as one, "You shall love the Lord your God with all your heart, and with all your soul, and with all your strength, and with all your mind; and your neighbor as yourself" (Luke 10:27). This commandment, which is taken from Deuteronomy 6:5 and Leviticus 19:18, sums up what we are called to as human beings and children of God.

Matthew 25 makes clear that loving God and loving neighbor are not two separate items on a list; rather, they are intertwined. Jesus says, "just as you did it to one of the least of these who are members of my family, you did it to me" (v. 40). Theologian Karl Rahner writes, "There is no love for God that is not, in itself, already a love for neighbor; and love for God only comes to its own identity through its fulfillment in a love for neighbor."[3] Sin, then, is missing the mark in relationship with God and neighbor.

What is the mark? Our aim is the future to which we are called, in which we love God and neighbor. This means that sin is dependent on grace. Had we never been called to be more, we would not have fallen short. Our target would be different—perhaps mere survival or even individual happiness but not loving relationship with God and neighbor. The gift of our vocation is the mark that we miss in sin, the path from which we go astray. In very practical terms, this means that all talk of sin is dependent on first acknowledging grace. "'Twas grace that taught my heart to fear. . . ." It is only in this context of God's love for humanity that talk of sin makes sense. The doctrine of sin is not a negative evaluation of humanity but rather a positive affirmation that we have a God-given vocation to love. Sin presupposes grace, not the other way around.

It is in describing how we go astray that the doctrine of sin offers a level of nuance that is not possible with our contemporary language of innocence and guilt based on individual moral choices. Traditionally, theologians have described human sin as both a state we find ourselves in and acts that we do. Humanity is tainted and infected with *original sin*, which is passed down in each generation, such that each human being also commits *actual sins*. The old-school version of this is familiar: Adam and Eve sinned, so every human person inherits a condition of sinfulness such that we all sin, too.

A more recent rendition—still in accordance with both the

Bible and mainstream doctrine—describes it in different terms. Each human being arrives into a world that is already fallen and relationships that are already broken. We can think of this in terms of social structures. Oppression and inequality—the very problems we've been examining throughout this book—were already in place when we were born. Humans miss the mark. Out of stupidity, selfishness, and short-sightedness, our attempts at being all we are called to be go off target. Sometimes we misunderstand the target altogether, imagining that self-aggrandizement is a better goal than love of God and neighbor. Along the way, we have created societies that are messed up at every level. We make violence an integral part of our economies, demonize people who are different from ourselves, and profit from harm done to others. Although it can feel like our particular historical moment is especially corrupt, a sturdy doctrine of sin reminds us that at all times and in all places, humans fall short of the glory of God: history and cultural anthropology bear this out. This large-scale mark-missing is *original sin*. We are born into a state of original sin; we inherit corruption. This is communal; it is a condition shared by the entire human race.

As we grow and develop within such fallen human communities, we are shaped and influenced by them. We learn their prejudices, imbibe their violence, and take on their misshapen values. By the time we are able to make free, individual, moral choices, we do so badly. Our freedom is compromised by our cultural conditioning, our individual choices take place in contexts determined by the larger society, our options are limited by unjust social structures, and even our moral compasses have been poorly calibrated in our sinful world. We retain our individual agency—our capacity to act—yet we are also bound by original sin. When we act out the implicit bias and distorted values of original sin, this is called *actual sin*. Although no one forces us to commit actual sins, the reality of original sin means that each of us will, inevitably, sin. Actual sins can be sins of commission (doing something that misses the mark) or omission (failing to seek the mark).

Our actual sins, in turn, contribute to the brokenness of humanity as a whole, adding to and sustaining original sin. Sin is, "in each the work of all, and in all the work of each."[4] The communal shapes the individual, and the individual contributes to the communal. Original sin results in actual sin, which contributes to original sin.

This way of looking at sin has profound explanatory power for the systemic problems in our common life, problems that are communal and structural as well as individual and particular. Racism is caused by original sin (the state of having missed the mark and broken relationship with God and neighbor) and it causes actual sin (particular actions of bigotry and prejudice that harm people of color). All the actual sins of particular instances of racism can be traced back to attitudes, structures, and assumptions created by the larger structures of white supremacy. At the same time, each of these particular, actual sins sustains and contributes to the original sin in which our culture is steeped. The actual sins of generations past—including conquest, colonization, and slavery—have become the original sin of the present. The racism that surrounds us—that shapes the life of every person in the United States—is part of the original sin that distorts our perceptions, thoughts, emotions, and behavior.[5]

This understanding of sin makes clear that we do not cease to be sinners when we come to faith. Unlike innocence and guilt, grace and sin are not mutually exclusive. Instead, sin is always dependent on grace. It is only because God has given us a target of loving communion with God and neighbor that our meanderings toward domination and fear are off-target. It is only because we have a higher calling and greater possibilities that our meanness is sinful. Grace—even the grace of salvation—does not remove us from the realities of communal brokenness and systemic injustice. Instead, grace keeps calling us forward to the future God intends. In the words of one Christian ethicist, "Salvation is the restoration of the goal that had been lost."[6]

This framework of grace and sin allows us to acknowledge the scope of our communal brokenness. It also reminds us at every turn that we are beloved children of God who are called to a better future. Our worthiness to be allies does not depend on a questionable claim to innocence but rather on our identity as persons created and called by God.

REPENTANCE

Shifting from a paradigm of innocence and guilt to one of grace and sin changes both how we understand the situation and how we respond to it. Most concretely, it shapes the steps forward for those of us who desire to be allies in the struggle for justice. The appropriate response to sin is repentance. The Greek word for repentance is *metanoia*, which indicates sorrow and contrition as well as a *change of direction* away from evil and toward God. As sin is missing the mark, repentance is acknowledgment that we are headed in the wrong direction and a turning toward the mark of our vocation, toward God. Because racism is sin, the very first step for white allies is repentance.

Repentance has two elements. The first is to acknowledge that the direction in which we are headed is off the mark. We cannot turn around until we admit we are moving in the wrong direction. The acknowledgment of structural injustice is a vital first step. Oppression thrives in denial. Christians can repent—openly acknowledge our communal brokenness and our personal participation in it—knowing that our sinfulness is neither the first nor the final word on us. We are beloved children of God, called to loving relationship with God and neighbor. We have missed the mark, broken relationships, and contributed to the harm of our neighbors and the earth. We, like every other person on the planet, fall short of the glory of God. Confessing sin is different than admitting guilt, for it does not separate us out from the innocent—sorting us into one group instead of another—but rather places us squarely in the midst of God's love for us despite our brokenness.

The second element of repentance is to move toward God. This is an active course correction. Repentance is not just a change of mind or a change of heart but also a change of action. We are not truly penitent if our acknowledgment of structural oppression does not come to fruition in action. It is tempting to confess the sin of racism and stop there, assuming that contrition and acknowledgment are enough. It is also tempting to act lovingly now, without acknowledging the sin that brought us to this place, and assume that is enough. Neither of these approaches qualifies as repentance.

FORGIVENESS

Repentance takes place in the context of grace and the assurance of God's forgiveness. Divine forgiveness is God continuing to be in relationship with us even after we miss the mark again and again. White people are, of course, already in relationships with black people, even if they are not personal or individual ones. We are deeply connected to one another as human beings, people living in this particular time and place, and as people with a shared vocation of love of God and neighbor. The relationships between white people and black people have been, and continue to be, broken in many ways. And yet we are still related to one another. Opting out of relationships across racial boundaries is not possible. The question, then, is how to heal our broken relationships. The concept of Divine forgiveness provides an overarching frame in which our damaged, cracked, and fragile relationships with one another are held together as we strive toward real community.

Forgiveness between people is often understood as one person giving up enmity toward another who has done harm. It indicates a change in the attitude and disposition of the one who forgives, but it does not necessarily entail continued relationship with the one who is forgiven. For example, a woman may forgive an abusive boyfriend while choosing to forgo any further relationship with him. Within the context of an abusive relationship, the decision to end a relationship can be an act of profound faith in which the survivor lays claim to her identity as a beloved child of God. Drawing such a boundary protects the woman from further harm and allows for her healing. Even after physical contact has ended, forgiveness may entail a refusal to continue putting energy (including that of anger or hatred) into a relationship.

Divine forgiveness is different. God does not need such boundaries to be protected from harm. Put simply, God is very big and we are very small.[7] And God chooses to stay in relationship with humanity even when we turn away.

In the Hebrew Bible, God calls the ancient Israelites into a covenant relationship. God tells the Israelites, "I will take you as my people, and I will be your God" (Exod. 6:7). Again and again, the ancient Israelites "miss the mark" and break covenant with God, by such actions as worshiping idols or behaving unjustly. At different times, God both chastises the people and punishes them, but God does not break relationship with them. When they fail to follow God's commands, the whole community is not cut off from God. There is always a way back into right relationship with God, be it through a ritual offering or another form of repentance. God remains steadfast in relationship with God's people. This continued relationship is the substance of forgiveness. When the people of ancient Israel turned away from God, God did not stop calling the people to God's self.

This is the good news and the bad news. This calling—this vocation—includes commandments and commitments. When the people turn from God, they are not released from these obligations. God's persistence in relationship both requires and enables the people to mend their ways. Psalm 139 questions, "Where can I go from your spirit? Or where can I flee from your presence. If I ascend to heaven, you are there; if I make my bed in Sheol, you are there. If I take the wings of the morning and settle at the farthest limits of the sea, even there your hand shall lead me, and your right hand shall hold me fast" (vs. 7–10). God will not abandon us; but neither will God let us off the hook!

In the New Testament, God enters into relationship with humanity in a different way, through the incarnation. Jesus is Emmanuel—God with us—and shows once more the patterns and possibilities of right relationship with God and neighbor. Humanity did what we do—that is, we sinned and turned away from God. The depth of human sin resounds in the cross of Christ. Yet in the resurrection, the life and ministry of Jesus Christ is vindicated as a true vision of the new creation, God's persistent love for humanity triumphs over sin and death, and God refuses to let us go.

Again, this is the good news and the bad news. It means there is still opportunity for us to fulfill our calling, and it means that we do not get to simply opt out of this vocation. The demands on us—to love God and neighbor—do not cease simply because we have failed to live up to them in the past.

The Bible makes clear that love and justice are essential aspects of Christian faith—not simply as ideals to believe in but as concrete practices that shape our lives. This means that all Christians are called to be allies. Lives differ dramatically and everyone has personal struggles; some people will not be able to become involved in political activities because they are dealing with illness, trying to make ends meet, or caring for an aging parent. Prayer is also important to the work of liberation, and in such situations prayer might be the perfect contribution.

For those of us who have the possibility in our lives to actively participate in the struggle for racial justice, it is important to recognize that such work is not an optional, extra activity that is extraneous to a life of faith. It is an integral part of Christian faith. When various factors make it difficult to become an ally—including segregation and guilt—we are called to overcome these obstacles.

This stubborn, persistent, unyielding call to love is what divine forgiveness looks like. It does not mean that our sins are wiped away as if by magic. Nor does it mean that we should continue to turn away. Instead, it means that God keeps calling, demanding, commanding, and loving us, continuing in relationship with us. There is a way for us to move toward right relationships with God and neighbor, no matter what our past has been, and we are called to make that move now, through repentance. In the same way that sin only makes sense in light of grace, repentance only makes sense in light of forgiveness—that is, God's continued call to us despite our turning away.

Again, this discussion is of divine forgiveness rather than interpersonal forgiveness. Unlike innocence and guilt, grace and sin are theological terms that always center on God. While repentance involves turning around and acting differently in order to better love our neighbors, the forgiveness on which the possibility of repentance rests is the forgiveness given by God. Put more simply, nothing said here implies that it is the work of those who have been oppressed to forgive those who have benefited from their oppression.

At the same time, it is the larger context of God's persistence in relationship that provides the ground for allies to stay in the struggle even when things go awry. Our commitment to justice is not based on one friendship that might, or might not, survive over time. Nor is it rooted in newly formed collaborations with other justice workers. Instead, our commitment rests in God's call to us, God's will that we be in loving relationships with God and one another. No matter how profoundly we mess this up, God keeps calling us. God does not give up on us, or on justice.

RECONCILIATION AND REPARATIONS

Two words come up often in discussions about how to move toward better relationships between white and black people in the United States. The first of these is reconciliation. Reconciliation between racial groups—understood primarily as togetherness, unity, and embracing diversity—has been a cherished goal of many activists since the civil rights movement and has been embraced by a number of Christian communities. This plan to live in harmony, celebrating our diversity and treating one another as equals, has not materialized. Such right relationships between blacks and whites cannot happen without understanding that the very concept of race was constructed in order to benefit whites at the expense of people of color.[8] White people and black people cannot simply play nicely together as equals because whiteness was invented to facilitate the subjugation of black people. Disavowing white supremacy in the present day is not enough to undo its ongoing structural and systemic harm. To move forward, we must first understand what has happened in the past, and then we must repair what we can of the damage done.

One way forward is to exchange the goal of reconciliation for that of reparations. Reparations means, quite simply, to repair the harm done and alter the structures in our common life so that the patterns of racism are not continued. In legal and political contexts, reparation indicates that a person or group who has taken the property, labor, or goods of another person or group must repay them for the loss. In the United States, the labor of enslaved Africans and African Americans was used to build a tremendous amount of wealth, while those enslaved were denied any portion of it. Some, having been enslaved and then gained their freedom, sued individual slave-holders or municipalities for compensation for lost wages.[9] In 1969, the National Black Economic Development Conference (NBEDC) endorsed the

"Black Manifesto," a document that called for concrete, material reparations of "$500,000,000 from the Christian white churches and the Jewish synagogues."[10] This was roughly equal to $15 for every black person in the United States and was to be allocated to various pursuits, including: "a southern land bank, publishing and printing industries, audio-visual networks, a research skills center, a training center . . ." and so on.[11] In retrospect, these demands were quite restrained. At the time, they were rejected by Christian organizations with various degrees of zeal. Even those groups that began investing money "for initiatives geared toward the well-being of Black Americans" spurned the language of reparations.[12]

The United States has paid reparations in the past, notably to Japanese Americans who were held in internment camps during World War II. However, the term "reparations" sparks outrage for many, who assume this would entail taking assets away from poor and middle-class white people. This assumption has been nurtured by politicians from all parties refusing to consider viable options for making reparations. A bill to study reparation proposals—just to consider what might be possible—has been introduced to congress every year for a quarter century. The bill never made it to the House floor for a vote.[13]

Such refusals to even consider reparations come from fear and not faith. Right relationship does not diminish anyone but rather provides for the flourishing of all. Clinging tightly to the benefits of white supremacy, rather than aiming for the goal of loving relationship with God and neighbor, is substituting human ideas of the good for Divine promises of abundance. It is missing the mark.

Deciding how we go about repairing our societal structures will require creativity and faith. And we cannot truly repent without doing this vital work. To turn away from the sin of racism and toward right relationship will require actively addressing the structures that maintain and continue oppression. Even though reparations of any kind cannot undo the damage of racism, the process of making reparations would fundamentally change the United States. "An America that asks what it owes its most vulnerable citizens is improved and humane. An America that looks away is ignoring not just the sins of the past but the sins of the present and the certain sins of the future."[14] Reparations would improve the culture of the United States in ways that exceed any particular material repair. Christians must embrace a reparations paradigm, and doing so might be a step toward the longed-for reconciliation.[15]

In the previous pages we have discussed the social construction of race and its historical moorings and ongoing destruction. We have analyzed racism through the theological lens of grace and sin, which points us toward the need for repentance. Christian repentance includes two elements: (1) an acknowledgment of brokenness and particular harm to relationships and (2) a turning away from such harm, back toward the vocation of loving God and neighbor. Repentance is not a one-time event but rather an ongoing aspect of a life of faith. In the next chapter, we will address concrete, specific ways to work for justice in our common life.

DISCUSSION QUESTIONS

1. Why do people feel overwhelmed when thinking about the problems of injustice in our society? Why do those feelings make it harder to engage effectively in the search for a better society?

2. What are the limitations of the categories of innocence and guilt in relation to societal problems?

3. The authors assert that God calls us to right relationships with God, with each other, and with the earth. This calling is grace.

Sin is when we miss the mark and get off track. Are these definitions of grace and sin familiar or unfamiliar?

4. Is the best response to racial inequality reconciliation or reparations? Could reconciliation be a result of reparations? What might reparations look like? Should the United States undergo a Truth, Reconciliation, and Reparation process, facilitated by faith or civic groups, at the local, state, and national levels?

CHAPTER THREE

Resources for Being an Ally

Many of us would like to heed a higher calling and contribute to making our communities more just and equitable. But it is very hard to know where to start and how to proceed. We are afraid that our efforts will be awkward or unwittingly offensive, and we have seen others embarrassed by their own missteps. Maybe we need some guidelines to go forward. The pages ahead will offer concrete advice on how to be an ally and a coconspirator for justice, drawing explicitly on the wisdom of our activist advisors introduced at the beginning of the book.

A list of rules and regulations, no matter how expansive, can never cover every possible situation. More than "dos and don'ts," we need explicit values that can be applied across circumstances. Although the specifics of our present troubles are unique, Christians have struggled with how to live toward our calling from the very beginning. In the first letter to the Corinthians, the apostle Paul gives a conflicted community advice that still resonates. After reminding the members of the church that there are many different ways to contribute to the upbuilding of the community, Paul writes, "And now faith, hope, and love abide, these three; and the greatest of these is love" (1 Cor. 13:13). These are three abiding values of Christian traditions that shape the way forward, referred to in some traditions as the "theological virtues." A virtue is a disposition, or posture, of the whole person toward that which is good. It is a way of being in the world that, in different circumstances, moves toward the mark of love of God and neighbor. Some traditional Christian virtues offer wisdom particularly useful today, including humility, prudence, fortitude, temperance, and patience.

FAITH

Many of us have a sense that what we see around us—the violence, suffering, and meanness in the world—is not how things ought to be. We look at the things that give immense material benefits to individuals in our society—money, power, prestige—and believe that these are not the highest values of humanity. There are more important things, such as kindness, compassion, and honesty. This is, already, a kind of faith. It is an affirmation that the meaning of the universe does not easily align with the things one can get away with in a given society. There is meaning that is stronger, or deeper, or longer lasting than self-interest. Whenever we let that meaning—in whatever way we glimpse it—be the North Star guiding our lives, there is faith. When we are honest, despite knowing that we wouldn't get caught in the lie; when we are compassionate, although no one would blame us for indifference; when we are kind, even though it will go unnoticed—this is faith. In this book, we have looked to, and from, Christian traditions to understand this calling toward a better way of being together.

In Christian teaching, faith is a living relationship of trust with the God we know in Jesus Christ, the God we learn about in Scripture and understand in the light of community, tradition, and experience, guided by the Holy Spirit. This faith provides both the impetus to work for justice and the vision of what justice looks like. Faith also offers assurance that whatever we contribute to the struggle—no matter how small—will not be in vain. Every opportunity to conspire for justice is an invitation to be part of what God is up to in the world.

Furthermore, faith in God helps us persevere in this work. While human efforts alone falter, the spirit of God will not. The Rev. Dr. Wil Gafney, an Episcopal priest and seminary professor, says that her "faith in God and Her redemptive power" sustains her activism in Black Lives Matter (BLM) and her work for inter-religious support in the United States. Gafney's faith helps her believe "in the inherent goodness of folk despite the evidence" and "that we can change the world for the good."

HOPE

Precisely because we have faith in God, we have hope that God's creative love will have the last word. We have hope that the vision of a future of right relationships—that future we remember in Scripture and in the life of Jesus Christ—will be realized. Rooted in different elements of Scripture, images of the future indicate a great communion of all persons, with God and with one another, in which all are loved and nourished.

We hope for this. Christian hope is not wishing or dreaming but rather acting in faith toward a reality that is promised but not yet seen. Rev. Dr. Lewis Brogdon, a pastor and scholar, writes of his own work for racial justice: "The . . . vision of the heavenly banquet sustains me. When all God's children gather together, we will be together in a way that is different from the ways we gather here on earth. So I pray that heaven's vision of fellowship comes incrementally in the work that we do here on earth."

In the same way that grace reveals our sin, a Christian vision of the future that God intends for us brings all the ways in which we fall short of this goal into stark relief. It makes us discontent with the status quo. "Hope has two beautiful daughters; their names are anger and courage. Anger at the way things are, and courage to see that they do not remain as they are." This statement, attributed to Augustine of Hippo, asserts that hope creates outrage and demands action. When great harm is done repeatedly to a community, as it is in our nation when transgender teens are attacked and black youth gunned down, grief and anger can be expressed in demonstrations and protests. This anger can be rooted in faith—in the sense that there is a greater meaning being denied in the systems that steal the lives of children. Anger can be an expression of hope—a profound sense that we are called to a different way of being together. While there are forms of fury fueled by hatred, zeal for justice is powered by a stubborn sense that things ought to be, could be, and will be better. Christian hope is "angry for a better world."[1]

LOVE

This vision of a better way of being together is, in Christian traditions, characterized by love. The idea that God is Triune communicates that the giving and receiving of love is absolutely fundamental to who God is. In creating, God invites others into relationships of giving and receiving love. First John 4:16 says, "God is love, and those who abide in love abide in God, and God abides in them." God's love transcends all socially constructed categories. Activist Rex Fowler describes the activity of an ally as precisely this, "to love across the artificial boundaries that society erects."

In concrete terms, this means that advocacy should always be about relationships. Nyle Fort, a community organizer and BLM activist, says that "simply going to a march is good, but it is not enough. Allies need to do the consistent, nitty-gritty work of relationship building." As we have already seen, the centrality of relationship can make some forms of advocacy easier than others. Many straight people become LGBTQ allies when they learn that someone with whom they were *already* in relationship (a child, sibling, or coworker) is LGBTQ. The reality of segregation in the United States means that many white people are not in close relationships with people of color.

Becoming an antiracist ally might not be the result of relationships but the beginning of relationships. That's OK, too. For some of us, activism can be the beginning of desegregating our lives, because the work might lead us to a different part of town and into a different community. We can, in the words of Ludger Viefhues-Bailey, "Develop true friendships that go beyond the struggle." This does not mean that personal friendships are the goal of allyship (that is, having black or LGBTQ friends does not mean your work is done), but rather, that in "loving across boundaries" we undercut the segregation and separation on which oppression thrives.

Many white people in the United States, particularly in rural areas, live in places with very few people of color. In our digital age, this is not an insurmountable obstacle. There are many ways online to connect with activist organizations and build relationships. If possible, it is important to be physically present as an ally, but a commitment to relationship can be manifest in other ways. Rev. Dr. Valerie Bridgeman, an activist for both LGBTQ equality and BLM, advises, "Get in the work. Do it. Don't just talk about it. Find the place of your passion and start building relationships."

Relationships are one of the great blessings of being an ally. Activist Jim Haber says that what sustains him in his efforts are "the amazing people [he has] met while working for social change and justice." More than just connecting with individuals, Jim feels connected to, "people all over the world . . . who are working for justice." Other activists, such as Rex Fowler, note that some of the steps of solidarity that enable entering into relationship with "those being treated unjustly" also enable Christians to "better enter into relationship with God."

These three virtues—faith, hope, and love—are steady guides for all forms of allyship and advocacy. There are many entryways into allyship. Rev. Joshua M. Pawelek, a Unitarian Universalist minister who has been involved in activism for LGBTQ rights and for BLM, throws the doors wide open with a list of ways allies can be useful:

> providing space for meetings, providing resources (money, food, buildings), supporting nonviolent civil disobedience, writing and delivering testimony, lobbying, writing letters to the editor, engaging in community organizing, doing public speaking, taking seriously the words and deeds of marginalized and oppressed people and not letting them face their struggles alone. There's a lot more, but this is the beginning of it.

Any small act toward justice is worthwhile. Furthermore, the difference between doing nothing and doing something is enormous. The most important thing is to do something. While the virtues of faith, hope, and love will serve as general guidelines, there are more specific suggestions. Some other traditional Christian virtues are especially useful for becoming an ally.

HUMILITY

Several of our activist collaborators encouraged allies to be humble, particularly in regard to learning. Humility includes not overestimating one's place in the universe.[2] One of the insidious effects of white supremacy is that all of us who live within its purview have been taught to see white people as the center and the norm. The vast majority of books assigned in grade school, high school, and even college, are written by white people. As whites identify with these authors, we unconsciously begin to believe that white people are the ones who narrate and describe reality. When we turn on the television, go to the movies, or watch the news, we often see white people as the center of the plot, the ones who decide what happens next and describe what is important. The messages of whiteness as the norm are pervasive. For those of us who are white, this means we have been taught to see ourselves as the center of the universe and the center in any given situation. Stepping into a context of antiracism means listening to what the world looks like from different perspectives and learning that our own perspective is not universal. Rev. Dr. Lewis Brogdon states,

> It is hard to get allies to even acknowledge that they have a lot of homework to do. They have lived and worked in a world that's told them they are the center. A part of justice work is de-centering privileged people and inviting them to live in a world they share with others. If they are interested in living in this kind of world, then they need to know that they have a lot to learn about others.

As allies, we must begin by learning about the day-to-day experiences of people who are not in the dominant culture. We must learn how interactions with the police unfold when the person pulled over is African American. We must learn about the obstacles faced by LGBTQ adolescents. We have to, in effect, relearn the world. This means we must listen to those with whom we wish to be allied. We must listen, believe, and grapple with realities that may be new to us. Often, the first impulse is to ask a person of color or an LGBTQ person to teach us. The trouble with this is that teaching is work. In effect, when a white person asks a black person to explain these things, this is a request for unpaid labor. People of color or people who identify as LGBTQ then have the multiplied burdens of surviving oppression, working for justice, and educating ignorant white or straight allies. Rev. Dr.

Bridgeman says, "It can be tiresome, as a black woman, to be in the 'teaching' role for white allies. . . . It's tiresome." Therefore, part of the role of a white ally is to be ready to learn but not ask others to teach. Ludger Viefhues-Bailey, active in movements for LGBTQ rights and racial justice, says, "I desire to learn humbly, without putting pressure on another to teach me."

If this sounds like a terrible bind, it isn't. Reading is the key. Authors who are African American, LGBTQ, and many, many others have written more than any one person could read in a lifetime. In written words, these authors have given a great deal of teaching to all of us. We can read about the experiences, histories, and perspectives of others. This does not mean just reading about racism and heterosexism. People of color and queer people have written about millions of topics. Whatever interests you—history, gardening, airplanes, fiction, botany, mysteries—someone who is not white has likely written about it. A library holds a key to new perspectives on reality.

In terms of current events, it is incredibly useful to avail oneself of alternative news sources. Mainstream media often presents a white, heteronormative point of view. Yet, there are many excellent news sources available online that present reporting, analysis, and commentary from different perspectives. Possibilities include www.theroot.com, http://twib.today, the podcast This Week in Blackness by Elon James White, and columns by Black public intellectual Dr. Brittney Cooper

Reliable sources on social media can be another avenue for learning. Read blogs by LBGTQ people and people of color. Follow activist organizations online (such as Color of Change and SURJ) to keep informed regarding local events that are not covered by mainstream media and to learn about ways to be supportive.

Finally, for those who are media savvy, follow a few African Americans who speak out for justice on twitter (@SonofBaldwin, @WilGafney, @deray, and many others). Then follow some of the people they follow; then follow a few more. Twitter becomes an avenue to learn different ways that Black people are engaging and interpreting the world. As many of you may know, it is an eye-opening educational experience to compare a live twitter feed of a protest or an incident involving police and mainstream news coverage of the same event. All of this—listening, reading, looking for different news sources, and being involved in social media—is part of what Wil Gafney calls "self-education."

The virtue of humility does not mean that we cannot learn from those with whom we ally ourselves. Instead, it points back to the idea of relationship. We should neither imagine that we are the teachers nor demand that others teach us. Rather, within the context of real relationship, after we have done some of our own work, we can learn from one another. Rex Fowler says, "Be in genuine, humble learning relationships, looking for opportunities to receive as well as give knowledge."

One key element in this humility is to not assume that we, as allies, know the best way to proceed in the work for justice. People in the dominant culture are often taught to be leaders. In the same way that we are taught the perspective of white people is the norm, we are taught that our ideas, skills, and ways of working are the best. This is exacerbated by class inequalities, which are so closely linked to racism in the United States. Given the economic effects of generations of racism, often the white people in a room full of social justice advocates will have more formal education than the black people in the room. Without intending to—without even realizing we are doing it—we can walk into a room and take over. At the very worst, non-humble allies imagine themselves to be saviors who swoop in to save those who cannot save themselves. More often, we tend to talk too much, imagine we have the best plans and ideas, step into leadership positions, and place ourselves in whatever limelight is available. This is problematic on many levels, as it reproduces the hierarchies of oppression we are hoping to subvert. Also, many of us do not yet understand the realities faced by people of color and people who are LGBTQ. And even if we've learned a bit, most of us have spent less time in the actual work of justice. As allies, we need to listen first and, in the words of scholar Amy Plantinga Pauw, "be willing to work behind the scenes on the invitation of others."

For those of us who are new to being allies, this is fantastic. It means we do not need to know everything to get started. We don't need to be able to lead a movement in order to be involved in one. If we have the humility to show up and do whatever is needed—be it making sandwiches, setting up chairs, or painting posters—there is room for us to be involved. If we can write a letter, stuff an envelope, walk down the street, or take out the trash, there is ample opportunity to be part of the civil rights movement taking place right now. In any city in the United States, an Internet search can reveal organizations that are already at work for justice. Find out who they are, where and when they meet, and then show up and get to work. Again, those who live in less densely populated areas might have a different task. It might be that in a particular small town, there is no group already active. In that case, an ally might need to start something that addresses the oppression of LGBTQ or African American people. It could be a book group, a lunchtime conversation, a monthly movie night, a Sunday school discussion, or five friends agreeing to read *The Root* along with the local paper. Just do something!

Rex Fowler, who runs the Hartford Community Loan Fund,[3] is exploring the possibility of creating a student loan refinancing fund for recent college graduates who are overburdened with educational debt. Many white college graduates are able to get help from their parents or grandparents to refinance their student debt—which lowers monthly payments and grants bankruptcy protections—by tapping into home equity or other assets. As discussed in chapter two, black Americans were denied access to FHA mortgages for thirty years and more recently steered into subprime mortgages. One effect of these policies is that black college graduates are less likely than white graduates to have home equity in their families' home that could allow for refinancing. A student loan refinancing fund would afford black college graduates, and others from low-income families, access to student debt refinancing. It would also offer a concrete opportunity for white people to help overcome some of the present day effects of a previous racist policy from which they may have benefitted.

Whether you are making coffee for a long-established organization or just starting up something in your own town, the virtue of humility remains the same. Joshua Pawelek explains,

> People of marginalized and oppressed identities will always, at some level, understand their struggles and what is needed better than you will. Even if you are the leader, you need to listen to their stories, believe their stories, take their stories seriously, and design your actions based on what they say they need, and in collaboration with them, not based on what you think they need.

PRUDENCE

The term "prudence" isn't very popular in the twenty-first century, but its delineation as a virtue goes back to roughly 400 BCE.[4] As understood and adapted by Christian traditions, prudence refers to wisdom in discerning which actions are appropriate in a given time and place. In the context of struggling for justice, prudence is a virtue that encourages allies to discern carefully where the focus of their energies should be.

Quite often, the role of allies is not to teach, enlighten, speak for, or represent those who are oppressed. Instead, our primary role is to go back to the spaces we already occupy within dominant cultures and advocate for justice there. It would be imprudent for a white man to take on the task of educating black men about racism or speaking for black men in public spaces. Instead, prudence dictates that a white man's role would be to educate other white people and to amplify the voices of black speakers in contexts where they might not otherwise be heard. In the words of Rev. Dr. Lewis Brogdon,

> Allies help by challenging the beliefs, values, and practices that support injustices in places marginalized persons rarely have access to. Allies can challenge ignorance, bigotry, indifference, and hatred in intimate relationships, family relationships, professional circles, and churches. Allies courageously speak truth to those close to them and use their privilege to foster compassion for others.

Valerie Bridgeman uses the memorable phrase "go get your cousins" to encourage white allies to work, first and foremost, to educate and influence other white people on issues of racism and injustice. Nyle Fort asserts that "one of the most important things white people standing in solidarity can do is to organize white communities."

This is, in many ways, the logical outcome of the humility discussed above. If we recognize our own need to learn and we do not demand that those who are oppressed be our teachers, then we need to learn and to educate ourselves and one another. Furthermore, our position in dominant cultures allows us access to spaces and conversations in which marginalized persons are not always welcome. Inside those spaces, we can, to use an activist's term, "amplify" the voices of those with whom we are allied. Jim Haber encourages allies to "speak to other people from our group about our perspective while encouraging people to listen to the people who are suffering more and more."

Although it ought not be necessary, such work can help those in the dominant culture appreciate the humanity and dignity of marginalized people they do not know. Dr. Ludger Viefhues-Bailey recalls that "early on in the LGBTQ liberation movement

. . . mothers of gay or lesbian people helped to humanize us in the eyes of the majority society." By standing with and for their children through organizations such as PFLAG, these family members refused the stigmatization of LGBTQ people. They educated the dominant culture and helped to bridge the gap created by ignorance, prejudice, and fear. Rev. Dr. Lewis Brogdon writes, "One way to counter injustice is to humanize people. People with privilege have distorted beliefs about marginalized persons. Some have never had close personal interactions with them."

In a society where people are often encouraged to think in us-versus-them categories, allies not only connect "us" and "them," they also make clear that the categories themselves are problematic. Jim Haber asserts, "the cognitive dissonance that the ally represents in the liberation struggle is vital to persuading more of the dominant group to see the light." Early in the struggle for LGBTQ liberation, the media narrative placed LGBTQ people and heterosexuals as opposing sides. The presence of allies, such as the parents involved in PFLAG, helped change this narrative by refusing this opposition. According to Frank O'Gorman, "Allies helped to change the debate from straight vs. gay to discrimination vs. equality."

If the largest part of prudence is to "get our cousins" rather than attempting to "save" those who are oppressed, another part is discerning when the privilege afforded us as members of dominant communities can be leveraged in support of marginalized groups. While allies should not seek the spotlight, it would be foolish to miss an opportunity if we are already in one.

The Rev. Dr. Marilyn McCord Adams, a theologian and philosopher, started teaching a Bible study at Trinity Episcopal Church in West Hollywood in the late 1980s. Because of the presence of some openly gay priests as volunteers in the church, gay men felt welcome. McCord Adams had been told, as so many are, that same-sex love is not consonant with Christianity, so she was unsure how to proceed. She remembers, "I asked myself,

What do I really understand about sexuality? I concluded, not much; it's a hard topic. I decided I had to be empirical, to keep my eyes open, ask lots of questions, and learn as much as possible. Turning to what I knew about God, I concluded, God loves each person God has made."

This was the beginning of decades of work for justice for the LGBTQ community. McCord Adams ministered to homeless men in Hollywood during the height of the AIDS epidemic and steadfastly advocated for LGBTQ liberation in every context in which she found herself, including as a professor at Yale Divinity School. In 2003, she became the Regius Professor of Divinity at Oxford University, an extremely prestigious position that commands attention in both academic circles and the Church of England. McCord Adams's appointment coincided with international controversy and debate among the global Anglican communion on the issue of whether or not same-sex love was to be regarded as sinful.

Soon after her arrival in England, McCord Adams was invited to preach at an Inclusive Church that supported LGBTQ equality. As she had been doing for twenty years, McCord Adams spoke a word of God's love to all people, regardless of sexual orientation. This time, however, her words garnered national media attention. She recalls, "I realized why I had been called to England. My chair brought automatic access to the press and national media." For the next six years, she gave speeches, wrote articles, organized, and generally used every bit of power and prestige she had to advocate for LGBTQ liberation. As a renowned scholar, an Episcopal priest, and a white person in a long-standing and happy heterosexual marriage, McCord Adams was buffered from some—but not all—of the professional retributions that could come from such strong work. "Basically," McCord Adams said, "allies are people who put the power and privilege they have to use for the benefit of people who either do not have it or cannot easily afford to exercise it in the situations in question."

While the willingness to stuff envelopes or make coffee is all that is needed to get started in the work for justice, as we build relationships with a particular community of struggle, we will identify places where our particular skill sets, assets, or opportunities overlap with what the community discerns as needs. It could be knowledge of local zoning codes, an available room to meet on Tuesday nights, a talent for catering, or a pickup truck to move supplies. Prudence helps us to offer what we have to the work at hand.

FORTITUDE

Another Christian virtue needed to be an ally is fortitude. While prudence helps us determine what actions to take, fortitude gives us the courage to take them, even and especially when doing so is difficult. It takes courage to do something new, be in new situations, learn new things, meet new people, and encounter the world in a new way. Joshua Pawelek is clear: "aspiring allies need to learn what it means to be courageous."

Listening to people who are oppressed will almost certainly hurt like hell. Building relationships across boundaries can exponentially increase the amount of love in your life, but it also increases the amount of vulnerability and grief. Loving other people isn't just risky; it comes with pain. There is a particular, added pain in loving people marginalized by your own culture. It can break your heart, repeatedly, to learn in detail the harms done in our society and the ways in which the people with whom so many of us have been taught to identify—white people, straight people, males, able-bodied people, middle-class people, and so forth—benefit from these harms.

There are strong temptations to respond to this heartbreak in one of three ways, two of which were discussed briefly in the previous chapter. The first is disbelief. We can make light of an event, refuse to see a pattern, or find a way to blame the person who was harmed—all in an effort to spare ourselves the pain of acknowledging the suffering of the oppressed. The second is defensiveness. We attempt to distance ourselves by declaring our own innocence. The third temptation is to shift the focus of attention from the injustice at hand to our feelings about it. This temptation can come out in long, heartfelt descriptions of sadness or guilt, the need to narrate one's own burgeoning awareness of oppression, or demands that those who are marginalized adjust their speech or tactics in order to make things easier for the white people in the room. However this happens, it re-centers white people instead of centering people of color. It also falsely equates the temporary emotional states of white people with the generational suffering of African Americans that is emotional, physical, psychological, material, and so on. It somehow imagines that it is harder for white people to learn about racism than it is for black people to experience it.

This phenomenon is called "white fragility." Valerie Bridgeman explains that aspiring allies hinder the work of justice "when they try to explain to people who are experiencing a particular societal pain that 'it's not really that,' or 'it's not that bad,' or 'you misunderstood,' etc. They also hurt when they start being defensive or making a 'thing' about them; when they are unable to hear something without inserting themselves into it." Even when learning the realities of oppression is painful, we are called to have fortitude. We can have conversations about our own feelings and experiences, but these should happen in contexts where our stories will not re-marginalize the voices of those who are oppressed.

Another reason we need fortitude is to face our own fears of offending others, both the people of color we are seeking to be allied to and our friends and families outside of justice work. Precisely because we do not ascribe to bigoted beliefs, we do not want to offend those who are marginalized. What if we say the wrong thing? Use the wrong term? There are two important things to remember in this regard. First, not doing anything is already offensive. Two, you will almost certainly mess up, so learn how to handle this.

Many of us were raised not to mention certain topics at the dinner table, including sex, religion, and politics. Often, the topics of race and sexual orientation were so far out of bounds that they did not even need to be mentioned as forbidden topics! Somehow, we imbibed a belief that it was more polite, and therefore less offensive, to never speak of these subjects at all. Many white people think we won't offend as long as we never mention race or anything race-related. This is simply not the case. Attempts to ignore race effectively ignore everyone and everything that is not white. Racism is a factor in every element of life in the United States.

Not discussing race does not make racism disappear, rather, it makes white people and white culture the only acceptable topic of conversation. Many white people do not notice when race and racism are not mentioned. However, people of color generally do. Many black people notice and see it for what it is: an erasure of everything that isn't about white people. Our silence on matters of race has been offending many people of color who witness it our entire lives. If no one told us how offensive we were being, it was only because we did not yet have strong enough relationships with people of color for them to let us know.

When we become antiracist allies, of course we start talking about race. But we are new at this, culturally ignorant, and generally clueless in many respects. So we mess up. And now, because we've started to build relationships, we are more likely to be in the room with someone who will tell us. This feels awful. As Marilyn McCord Adams said, "Being an ally is a tricky business, one in which it's easy to be clumsy and easy to wind up with egg on your face." When this happens, the way forward is quite straightforward, even if it does take courage. Apologize. The best apologies look something like this: "I'm sorry. Thank you for telling me that was out of bounds. I will try not to do that again." That's all that needs to be said, and then follow through on the promise and try not to repeat the offense. This is repentance in the most concrete of circumstances. Bridgeman assures us:

> It's inevitable that people screw up. . . . It's in all of our histories and DNA: white supremacy, patriarchy, sexism, racism, classism, heterosexism have long histories and deep roots—in us, in our families, in our cultures. We have to learn how to really repent (not just say "sorry" but change based on being called on it or discovering how we perpetuated it). And then we have to continue to lean into learning how to be free.

The flip side of this is when we've learned a little bit and can recognize when someone else makes a mistake, we let them know and, in the words of Amy Plantinga Pauw, "give them room to apologize." Rev. Osagyefo Sekou, a minister and social activist involved in the Black Lives Matter movement, makes a helpful distinction. He says that the goal is not to call people "out," but to call people "in."[5] We all make course corrections, again and again, as we press on toward the goal of loving God and neighbor.

Being an ally requires fortitude in a number of ways, because it is a life-changing endeavor. Frank O'Gorman advises, "Be prepared to have one's worldview turned upside down. Be OK with feeling uncomfortable. Be prepared to re-think one's sense of merit and achievement."

Lastly, being an ally demands fortitude because if you stand close to those who are oppressed, the forces of oppression often hit you, too. The privilege and benefits of being part of dominant cultures (white, straight, etc.) will not disappear, but the invisible vitriol that is the lifeblood of white supremacy and heterosexism will likely become apparent in surprising places. A number of friends, coworkers, and even family will reveal unsuspected levels of bigotry. When the work of allies begins to press on systemic points of injustice, in a school board or a city council or a church group, the intransigent power of structural oppression may push back. Rev. Dr. Lewis Brogdon encourages,

> Be strong because you will live in the middle of deep and painful divisions. You will often feel conflicted as you live and work in between people with privilege who refuse to acknowledge it and people who are daily marginalized by a vicious system. You will feel like you are being attacked by both and there will be days you wonder if it is worth it. My advice to you is be strong. You are making a difference.

TEMPERANCE

The virtue of temperance refers to guiding our own passions carefully through the use of reason. It is self-regulation. In the context of becoming an ally, temperance indicates the careful balance of one's own agency—one's ability to act— in the midst of a movement.

As discussed above, people from dominant cultures tend to assume they already have the necessary knowledge and to assume that their rightful place in almost any setting is that of "leader." The virtues of humility and prudence are helpful guides in steering allies away from these pitfalls and toward better ways of relating. Especially when one is new to a particular struggle, humble learning and doing the tasks identified as needed by the oppressed group are important. In fact, learning to follow the lead of a marginalized group is incredibly challenging for many aspiring allies. White people often advocate organizing without realizing that this means some people must be willing to be organized. Or, more likely, without imagining themselves in the role of "organized" rather than "organizer." Following the leadership of marginalized groups has proved so difficult for allies that an unfortunate philosophy of allyship has emerged that emphasizes the need for allies to "take leadership" from organizers from within the marginalized group with which they are allied. It is an important step in being an ally to learn to trust and to follow those who less often have access to leadership positions in our society.

However, the practice of "taking leadership" is also complicated. Activist and writer Jessica Stewart advises all allies to "follow the leadership of the community" with which they are making common cause for justice. At the same time, Stewart acknowledges that this can be tricky. One reason for the difficulty is that movements and marginalized communities are internally diverse. There are many different kinds of groups struggling for similar goals using different approaches, or perhaps even identifying quite different goals on the path toward justice. There are often different ideas, options, and methods within any one group. Stewart questions, "As an ally, how does one follow the lead of a conflicted community and engage with integrity?" This difficulty is examined in a powerful essay titled "A Critique of Ally Politics," whose author goes by the name M., which states that the dictate to take leadership "starts to get real complicated, real fast, however, as you discover that there is no singular mass of people of color—or any other identity-based group—to take guidance from, and that people within a single identity will not only disagree about important things but also will often have directly conflicting desires."[6]

At its absolute worst, a strict commitment to take leadership from others can be an abdication of responsibility for one's own actions and a false denial of one's own agency. We make choices about who to work with and how to do so within a context of varied groups and strategies.

Temperance is needed, because we are the ones who make the

decisions about how we struggle for justice. This involves learning from, and listening to, those with whom we are allied, as well as self-awareness about our own goals, values, and choices.

The Rev. Dr. Marilyn McCord Adams experienced the necessity of temperance in her work as an ally to LGBTQ persons. Leaders of the movement for LGBTQ rights in London were "glad to have the glitter of [her] title associated with their movement," and she was happy to be a "public champion" for the cause. However, at times conflicts between LGBTQ leaders in the movement left her feeling "hamstrung" by egos and politics, and on occasion organizations attempted to override her agency completely. She wrote, "They wanted to use me for their ends and assign me the roles (in one case, they even tried to tell me what to say in a speech)." When the agency of the ally is negated, by either the ally or members of the marginalized group, then the goal of relationship falls apart.

What is needed to be an ally varies depending on the situation. This is why the virtue of temperance, the cultivation of thoughtful self-regulation of our passions (including our passion for justice), is so important. Sometimes this means stepping back. Those who are oppressed might well set boundaries regarding the work of allies, and these boundaries should be respected. McCord Adams wrote, "Allies have to know when to take a back seat or drop out, while yet being ready to step back in if desires and situations change. *Allies have to be resolutely more committed to the cause than to their own roles in realizing its goals.*"[7]

At other times, temperance can mean stepping forward. Jim Haber advises allies "to cede much but not all of the limelight to the people who are standing up for themselves." There are moments, however, when the presence of an ally highlights new possibilities for our world. He writes, "As someone with white skin privilege, and as a Jew, and as a man, there are times [when I come into the limelight] when it isn't out of a sense of privilege or entitlement, but out of a sense of wanting to be part of a corrective, cognitive dissonance in which men stand by and with women; whites stand by and with people of color; Jews stand by and with Palestinians."

PATIENCE

It is impossible to overstate the importance of patience in struggling for justice. Not patience with injustice but rather what Nyle Fort calls it—"revolutionary patience" to engage in "long-distance organizing." Fort says that racism is "a 500 year old problem" and we "can't simply march or chant it away." The work of justice is not a sprint, not even a marathon, but something longer still. Stewart states that allies "should be steadfast in the pursuit of justice and dismantling oppression—in other words, commit for the long haul."

While we should not be patient with injustice, we should be patient with ourselves and with each other. One concrete way in which allies must be patient is in terms of our reception by marginalized groups. In particular, people of color often view any white person aspiring to be an ally with suspicion. This is not "reverse racism" because there is no larger structure that benefits people of color at the expense of white people. Neither is it exactly prejudice. Rather, it is the result of years of experience. In the United States, people of color experience an extremely large number of negative interactions with white people, which results in hesitance to trust white people.

Furthermore, people of color involved in the struggle for racial justice have encountered a lot of aspiring white allies who behaved badly, used their involvement in the movement for personal gain, or disappeared. This means our commitment to the work for justice must be patient, steadfast, and unwavering even when those we struggle beside do not yet trust us. Valerie Bridgeman writes, "You're going to be looked on with suspicion. And you're going to have to put your 'freedom fighter' card on the table time and again to prove you mean it. Get over that and just keep showing up and putting it on the table until you earn the right to be trusted."

Another issue that falls under the need for patience is this: LGBTQ people and people of color are just as intelligent, just as thick-headed, and just as sinful as anyone else. In learning to respect and love people who are different, it is important not to romanticize or valorize them. Getting involved in justice work will lead to meeting amazing people and to meeting people who are manipulative and mean-spirited. It takes discernment to figure out who is being rationally suspicious and who is being mean, to learn when we have unintentionally messed up and need to learn and when we have just encountered someone who is not nice. Patience is needed to persevere in the struggle in all its imperfections.

In Christian traditions, the virtues of faith, hope, love, humility, prudence, fortitude, temperance, and patience are ways of being in the world that we can cultivate and nurture through practice. They increase in us as we enact them over time, in as much as our embodiment of them is aiming at the future to which God calls us. As we live toward love of God and neighbor, these virtues guide us and grow in us. They are part of how we love, how we hope, and how we live in faith.

Christian values and virtues are also excellent guides to being an ally in struggles for justice. They will help us avoid some of the strongest temptations, so long as we are moving toward our calling. Bridgeman encourages us to get moving, right now:

> Get in the work. Period. Allies shouldn't "over study" or "over-think" the issues. Get into it. Build real relationships. Get close. Risk the pain and dirtiness of it all. Risk being rejected—by their current community and by the people they want to be connected to. Trial and error. Action and reflection. But if someone waits until they "get it" completely, they will always be on the sidelines.

DISCUSSION QUESTIONS

1. Which of the values or virtues that you were taught do you find most helpful in your own work for justice?

2. What are some of the concrete ways we express love of neighbor when we work for social justice?

3. What resources have you discovered for how to understand the struggles of persons of color and the LGBTQ community? Who are your conversation partners? What have you read that you find helpful?

4. Have you ever been uncomfortable discussing race with persons of color? Why was that the case? Have you found ways to become more comfortable with those conversations?

CHAPTER FOUR

Concrete Steps

AN EXERCISE

"What can I do?" is an important question for allies to ask, and one that can be intimidating. Here is a brief exercise designed to expand our thinking about what we can contribute to the struggle for justice.

Take a sheet of paper and draw lines on it that divide it into three sections. Label the first "Abilities." List ten things that you know how to do. Many of us think of our top-level abilities—the most complex and difficult things—as our primary abilities. For example: nursing, sales, teaching mathematics, and so on are top-level abilities. Listing as many as ten different abilities presses us to name some other abilities that are likely not part of our professional lives. These might include cooking, speaking a second language, basic home repair, babysitting, drawing, dealing with paperwork, and on and on. Once you get beyond your top-level abilities and begin thinking more broadly, you will find you have many more than ten abilities.

Label the next section "Assets" and list ten things in this column. Again, we often think first of top-level assets, such as a home or financial assets. Listing as many as ten encourages us to think more broadly and creatively. For example, a car is a very valuable asset. So is a lawnmower, a Costco card, a hands-free phone connection that allows you to make calls while doing housework, a kitchen table, and a printer. Time is a vital asset. Do you have five minutes a day to contribute? Is your schedule flexible, so that you could attend a meeting during the day or go with someone to a government office?

The third section of the paper should be labeled "Access." Here, list ten spaces to which you have access. What rooms or communities can you walk into with ease? There are likely several spaces you inhabit on a daily or weekly basis, such as your place of work, your place of worship, and perhaps a book club, a gym, or a service organization. Each of these is a space where you could bring concerns or ask for assistance. There are also other spaces that you perhaps don't enter often but where you would be admitted without question. This might include a school board meeting, a city council meeting, or a neighborhood association. An educated white man in professional attire can walk into many offices and be taken more seriously than a poor Latina immigrant would be. While we wish this were not the case, it is; so we recognize that some of us have more access than others, and we leverage it for justice.

None of these lists will be exhaustive; you have more abilities, assets, and access than will fit in these columns. However, the goal is to begin thinking broadly about what we can offer in the struggle for justice. In addition to knowing what we have to bring, it can be useful to know about particular forms of activism.

SIX WAYS TO STRUGGLE FOR JUSTICE

Connect

In a world with so many needs and so many populations that are oppressed or vulnerable, it can be very hard to know where to start. Any one person might intellectually and emotionally support a great number of struggles: for an end to an ongoing war, for bold action to deter climate change, for Palestinian rights, against bullying in schools, for a living wage, for education reform, and so on. These and other struggles are all interrelated and, in a fundamental way, one struggle. At the same time, if we feel equally pulled to each of these we might never offer concrete and active support to any of them! Generalized feelings of support (or fear, or despair, or worry) do not do a bit of good. Action takes place in the realm of particularity.

We each have to choose where to start. The starting point for any individual person often comes down to proximity. What struggle are you close to? Do you know a transgender teen who is suffering? Jump in there. Is your church sponsoring a refugee family? Great. Did your cousin's neighbor's ex-girlfriend mention an effort to prevent a pollution emitting plant being built in a poor neighborhood? That's close enough. If it is the case that no struggles cross your path, that no one in your life is marginalized, this is an indication that you need to occupy different spaces. Expand the circle of your daily life to include people of different racial backgrounds and economic circumstances. While that might take some courage, it will result in a broader and more beautiful world.

Whatever crosses your path or stays on your heart is a perfect beginning. Do not let an overabundance of choices keep you from participating in any particular struggle. Connect with a particular effort and with a particular community.

■　■　■

Martin's Story

"What does it mean to be an evangelical Christian and yet make room for other people's journey of faith?" This is the question near to Martin Brooks's heart. To address it, Martin connects. In Louisville, Kentucky, Martin has created a ministry of connecting Christian and Muslim communities, fostering genuine relationships in which people of different faiths can learn from and with one another. One of the programs Martin runs is a series of Peace Feasts. These are usually ethnically based. For a recent Feast, Martin invited a roughly equal number of Kentucky Christians and Somali Muslims to dinner at a Somali-owned restaurant. He then asked leading questions for people at each table to discuss. He started off by asking, "What is it about Islam that moves your heart and inspires you?" After a while, questions get more challenging, sometimes including issues of colonialism or drone warfare.

In the summer of 2015, Martin, working as the Midwest Regional Director of Peace Catalyst International, received a grant from First Christian Church of Louisville. The purpose of the grant, as explained by Pastor Brian Gerard, was to help the congregation form a dialogue and relationship with the River Road Mosque in Louisville. The first step in this process was an invitation for members of the church to attend worship at the mosque on September 18. On September 16, the mosque was vandalized with anti-Muslim graffiti. Many members of First Christian Church attended worship on the 18th. In addition, hundreds of people, from many faith traditions, came to the mosque that day. The city of Louisville presented the mosque with a Compassion Bench, in recognition of the work of kindness and compassion done by the Muslim community. A diverse and interfaith crowd of people from all over the city painted over the vandalism.

Although the relationship between First Christian Church and River Road Mosque was just at its barest beginnings, it was meaningful that these communities were already connected before the vandalism occurred. It enabled the congregation at First Christian to be better allies. The relationship between the two congregations continues.

■ ■ ■

Kristin's Story

"Don't reinvent the wheel," says Kristin Crinot, a business owner with well-honed organizational skills. In fact, it is much better if we don't. Humility requires that we learn from and work with those who are directly experiencing the effects of oppression. For any cause that calls to us, there are likely already groups and organizations up and running in the struggle for justice. To facilitate connections and collaborations, Crinot has developed an online platform called "The Ally Network" (www.theallynetwork.org). Currently operating in Louisville, the Ally Network website let's people interested in justice movements quickly learn what organizations are already active. It also allows various activist groups to post events on a shared calendar and thereby support each other.

If you live in a different place, a computer search and a few phone calls can connect you to people who already know about the particularities of this struggle and are welcoming to allies. The Black Lives Matter website (www.blacklivesmatter.com) has a link on its main page labeled "How You Can Help" and another labeled "Connect with Us." If you know you want to connect with a particular struggle, such as immigrant rights, but don't know what groups are already active, use a search engine and try typing "assisting" followed by the marginalized population and the name of your city. The search "assisting immigrants Louisville" pulls up three well-established and well-respected justice organizations with contact information. It is OK to call and ask how you can be a part of any group's efforts. If you call with a whole plan in mind, or with an assumption that you will be leading things, you will be met with suspicion. But if you call with a desire to be part of what the group is already doing, you will likely be well received.

While it is necessary to connect with a particular struggle within the larger movement toward justice, it is also important to see the intersections. In the United States, racism interacts with every other form of oppression. This means that the discussions and activities that are focused on a different particular issue should also involve reflection and action on race. For example, ecological concerns intersect with race because pollution-emitting facilities are more likely to be located in neighborhoods populated by people of color. At the same time, these neighborhoods often have fewer parks and greens spaces. If you find yourself connecting with a group that advocates for justice without reflecting on race, encourage discussion on this topic or find another group with which to work.

Amplify

Now that you are connected, in whatever form, to a group or organization that struggles for justice, part of the task is to amplify the voices, concerns, and insights of the oppressed. We increasingly live in a world of misinformation and disinformation, where people who are not explicitly connected with an oppressed group might never hear accurate reports of their struggles, let alone adequate analysis of the causes. As an ally, our work includes giving accurate information that we have learned from the oppressed in every circumstance possible. This includes social media, but more importantly it means talking about justice, and about race, in each of the spaces to which we have access. Suggest that your book group read a book written by a black person. Ask about racial differences in suspension rates at the PTA meeting. Bring what you are learning from others into the spaces you already occupy.

Those of us who are white have been taught not to mention race in polite company. While some might consider talking about race bad manners, it is necessary for good faith. If you haven't spoken openly about race before, it will likely feel uncomfortable at first. Do it anyway. Do it so often that you do not stumble on the words. Speak as if lives are at stake, because they are.

This does not mean you need to argue with your drunk uncle at Thanksgiving dinner or that you are morally obligated to change the mind of your recalcitrant aunt. However, it does mean that you must speak the truth at every table—even in your own family—to reject racism.

People will respond differently to your comments. Some will try to enforce the rules of polite white company and discourage you, in ways both subtle and overt. One of their tactics will be to ask why you think you are an expert. As much as you need humility when you are learning from the oppressed, you need boldness when you are speaking with those of the dominant culture. Rely on the wisdom you are learning and keep amplifying those voices, bringing them into spaces where they might not otherwise be heard.

Advocate

Advocacy is one of the most familiar types of activism. This is where we actively support policies and policy makers that will make society more just. The particular justice struggle that you connect with will raise up specific policy concerns, such as raising the minimum wage, changing sentencing guidelines, or resisting appointments of political figures. Advocating for these specific issues might include writing elected officials, calling elected officials, calling voters, attending meetings, marching in demonstrations, sending mailings to voters, or walking door to door to talk with people.

This is, in some ways, the easiest part of being an ally. It simply requires the willingness to do it. Put the phone numbers of your local, state, and national representatives into your cell phone. When you have five minutes—in a line, before a meeting, waiting to pick up your kids—call one of them and politely ask them to support (or reject) the specific policy that the justice group you are connected to has identified. Your call will likely be picked up by a low-level staffer. They will hear your concerns and write down that you called. You do not need to argue or persuade, just be specific about what you want and why. There are scripts available for how to make such calls. It helps to make such calls repeatedly. If you call today, call again tomorrow.

Email, postcards, and letters can be used in just the same way. The cumulative effect of such advocacy can be powerful, for it lets the representatives know that members of their constituency care about this particular issue and are paying attention to it.

January 2, 2017 was the day before a new session of Congress was to begin in which the Republican Party held control of both houses. Apparently in preparation for coming actions, House Republicans voted to "effectively kill the Office of Congressional Ethics," which served to ensure independent investigations of corruption in congress.[1] Americans responded by calling and e-mailing their representatives to demand that this be stopped. On January 3, congress members found "their offices inundated with angry missives from constituents."[2] Republican representatives "involved in the decisions have attributed the reversal to . . . a barrage of phone calls."[3]

On any given policy issue, our efforts might not bear fruit in the way we hope. However, over the long haul, they matter. They do create change. They also prevent things from being even worse. If oppressive policies are put into place when congress members receive 100,000 calls asking them not to support such policies, one can only imagine what the policies would look like if no one called at all. In the parlance of some church communities, the devil is an opportunist. If we, through our silence, signal that we are not invested in the lives of an oppressed group, the structural racism in our country will take that opportunity to increase.

Accompany

Accompaniment is a time-honored form of Christian ministry that can be adapted to almost any situation. It happens when a person who is part of the dominant culture is with a person who is oppressed. This has often been employed internationally, when white U.S. citizens travelled to El Salvador, Guatemala and other places to be with Christian pastors and activists who were threatened by agents of repressive government regimes. A local pastor who questioned the policies that left his congregation in dire poverty could easily be "disappeared," never to be heard from again. However, if that pastor were accompanied by a white person from another country, such a disappearance would fall under scrutiny from the international community.[4] The practice of "being with" offered a measure of aid and protection to those who were oppressed and a transformative education to those from the dominant community who then returned to their countries of origin to amplify the truth of what was happening.

Thankfully, traveling internationally to accompany an activist threatened by death squads is not the only form of accompaniment. There are many ways of accompanying those who are oppressed in the United States right now, today.

Start small. When you are in a public place, be friendly to people who look different than you. This sounds so simple as to be silly, but the combined effects of segregation and implicit bias mean that often when we are with people from another racial background we are not really *with* them at all. We don't engage. When we need to ask for directions, we ask someone from our own racial group. While there might be small talk between the white cashier and the white customer, small talk is far less likely if there is a racial difference between the two. It is not an insignificant thing to smile, to make friendly eye contact, to say hello, to chitchat with a stranger. Strike up a conversation in the checkout line, scoot over for another passenger on the train. Be present with and to people from marginalized communities.

This basic friendliness across lines of division helps set the tone for our society as a whole, refusing to normalize and accept the denigration of any social group. Not only is it pleasant, it is also a key step in preventing hate speech and harassment.

Bullies—cowards that they are—are less likely to target a person who is with a member of the dominant culture. A central element of bystander intervention (how to help if someone is being harassed) is to be *with* the targeted person, by talking with them, standing or sitting next to them, and focusing your attention on them.

Often we have impulses of friendliness or kindness toward another person or group across racial lines, but we are too afraid to act on them. We wonder: Would it be appropriate? Would it be offensive or laughable? For the record, basic acts of kindness are always appropriate, and it is the work of separation and segregation that keeps us from engaging in them more often.

After the presidential election in 2016, many communities feared for their safety. Hate crimes rose along with racist and xenophobic graffiti. In Louisville, Kentucky, the Americana World Community Center invited people to send in notes and cards to immigrants and refugees in the city, affirming "We're glad you are here" and "We stand by you." These letters are not enough, of course, but they are still valuable. When a community is assailed by hate, it is important to provide a message of love.

Another important form of accompaniment happens on a small scale within our cities. When a person from a marginalized community has to deal with government offices, or school officials, or almost any other kind of system, it can make a big difference to have members of the dominant culture with them.

■ ■ ■

Heidi's Story

Rev. Heidi Worthen Gamble works for the Presbyterian Church (U.S.A.) in Los Angeles. One powerful ministry of accompaniment Heidi works with is the Guardian Angels court watch program. The Guardian Angels help children refugees in deportation proceedings in U.S. immigration courts. These proceedings determine whether or not the children will be granted political asylum—or protection—in this country or if they will be deported back to the countries they are fleeing.

In certain areas of Central America, violent international gangs have significant power, in part due to U.S. involvement in the wars in the 1980s that devastated the economic infrastructure and left remnants of death squads in place, and in part due to more recent U.S. policies of deporting gang members. These gangs—which now hold more sway than local, regional, and even federal governments in the area—recruit young people, often threatening to kill parents and siblings if the targeted child refuses to join. Such horrific options lead mothers to send their children north in a desperate attempt to save them. This dynamic led to the surge in unaccompanied minors crossing the U.S. border in 2014. Most of these children are turned away. Those that are not immediately rejected are placed in detention centers or housed with relatives by the Office of Refugee Resettlement and must find legal representation to go before a judge to determine if they will be allowed to win political asylum, or protected status, in the United States.

This process is filled with obstacles, as children must navigate an unfamiliar legal process in a foreign language, including finding and paying for legal representation on their own. Under pressure from the government to move these kids through the process quickly, immigration judges sometimes run these cases so fast it is called a "rocket docket." Imagine a twelve-year-old being told by a judge that he must find a lawyer within two weeks or the deportation process will begin.

Heidi and the Guardian Angels work to *connect* these kids to pro bono legal service providers as well as to services that offer food and clothing. They *advocate* for these children by partnering with the National Lawyers Guild on a lawsuit demanding universal legal representation for children in this situation. Most important, the Guardian Angels *accompany* refugee children in the courtroom, protecting the children by holding the legal system accountable.

Volunteers in the program arrive at the courthouse in T-shirts with angels on them. As observers in the courtroom, they are not permitted to speak. However, they are very strategic about nonverbal communication. If the judge is rude, the Angels sigh and shake their heads. Using facial expressions and physical gestures, they communicate disdain if the children are treated poorly.

It is a simple form of ministry. They are with the children, and they make it clear to the judges that members of the dominant community (in this case, U.S. citizens) are paying attention to what happens. The results are breathtaking. The Guardian Angels have been active for over two years in Los Angeles. In that time, not a single trial where they have been present has resulted in deportation.

■ ■ ■

When marginalized groups engage in nonviolent protest, sometimes they invite allies to accompany them. The strategy of accompaniment has been used recently in Black Lives Matter protests.

Shannon's Story

After Michael Brown was killed in Ferguson, Missouri, the community cried out in mourning and anger. Before the protests were even protests—when they were simply communal lament—the police responded with an enormous show of militarized force. The young people of Ferguson were presented as violent looters. And yet the video footage of the nightly protests did not show violent riots—it showed young people being tear-gassed and shot with rubber bullets. It showed bruises and blood on the faces of youth; it showed tanks and military weapons on the streets of the United States, aimed at our own people. Like so many other people, I was distraught. One morning my son Jacob, who was fourteen at the time, came downstairs for breakfast and said, "Mom, I think we should go to Ferguson." I had the same feeling. Surely, if young people are being attacked, we should go to help. But I didn't know how to help. I said, "What could I do in Ferguson? I don't know how to fix this. I'm not a medic or a political leader. I know how to make sandwiches, not deal with this kind of crisis."

Two nights later, I was sitting in the auditorium of Jacob's high school, hearing details about a course of his, when I got a text from a friend I'd known since high school. Her message was short: I'm in STL. I texted back: Why? She responded that there was a call for clergy to accompany the young protesters. Perhaps police would be less likely to shoot rubber bullets at teenagers if there were people in clergy collars standing right beside them. My friend, Rev. Dr. Leslie Callahan, was going to march with the protestors. I texted back: I'm clergy.

The next day I drove to Ferguson. A lot of things fell into place to make that possible for me: I had a car, I could take the time off from work, my husband was happy to care for our children, I had friends in St. Louis who would let me stay at their home. What helped me make the decision to go was the fact that there was a clear invitation that I knew applied to me. I was clergy; there was a call for clergy. I could go. I did accompany the protestors, along with many other ministers from various religious traditions. I learned a great deal, and our presence did seem to lessen the violence.

What I realized much later was this: sandwiches would have been appreciated.

We all know what to do when someone experiences a loss— you bring food. It is a near universal sign of care for those who grieve. And yet somehow that seemed inadequate, and I did not think it would be appropriate in such serious circumstances. In retrospect, I know that delivering a platter of sandwiches to the church where the protestors were gathered would have been welcomed, and that a note of kindness and support would have been appreciated by people experiencing so much meanness. I had let the sense of difference, born out of segregation, prevent me from enacting basic Christian kindness.

■　■　■

There are many ways to accompany those who are marginalized or oppressed. It is vitally important to be in physical company with people who are struggling with injustice. But there are also other ways to be with people, and none of these are insignificant. For example, if the government began to require a registry by Muslims, it would be a powerful form of accompaniment for people of all faiths and people who are not religious to register as Muslims. Earlier in this book, we noted that dividing people by racial categories has been a means of social control in our country, a way for those with money and power to prevent the kind of solidarity that fueled Bacon's Rebellion. Accompaniment says clearly: we will not be separated.

Impede

Learning to respect authority and do as we are told is part of growing up. It is necessary for a child to submit to a parent's wisdom ("Don't play with matches!") and go along with the rules of elementary school ("Sit on the mat for story time"). As we get older, we are both encouraged to question authority and expected to acquiesce to it on a daily basis. Our acquiescence is motivated by a mixture of common sense and fear. If we all stop when the light is red, then we will arrive at our destinations more safely. If someone doesn't stop at a red light, he might get a ticket.

When it comes to systemic injustice, our tendency to acquiesce to authority is problematic. We can easily go along with an unjust situation or demand out of habit, without considering other options.

Christian ethicist Miguel De La Torre reflects on communities near the southern border of the United States who are faced with manifestly unjust immigration policies and practices. Activists in this struggle employ all of the strategies above, including advocacy to change the policies. However, given that the policies are not yet changed, they also work to slow down the implementation of the current, unjust practices. De La Torre refers to this as "an ethics *para joder*."[5] It is a kind of holy mischief that throws a wrench into unjust systems. For Harry Potter fans, this might resonate with the spell *Impedimentia!* While the goal is to change unjust policies and practices, it is also valuable to slow down their working in the meantime.

Some of the strategies mentioned above also fall into this category. For example, calling elected representatives every day is a form of advocacy, but it also slows things down in the office as staffers must devote time to answering calls. For Christians to register as Muslims would be a form of accompaniment, but it would also impede the workings of such a registry.

Impeding happens on large and small scales. A website launched recently asks students to "expose and document" professors who "discriminate against conservative students, promote anti-American values and advance leftist propaganda in the classroom."[6] The list at this point features academics who address racial injustice and believe that religious diversity is valuable.[7] Several students and professors are attempting to impede this kind of targeting by submitting professors who are fictional or historical. Others are self-reporting as a point of pride. The website might continue, but these allies are going to make it take a lot of effort.

■ ■ ■

Alison's Story

Rev. Alison Harrington is Pastor of Southside Presbyterian Church in Tucson, Arizona, a congregation with a rich history of impeding injustice. This church is part of the sanctuary movement.

While the concept of sanctuary—a place of worship functioning as a refuge—goes back to biblical times, the modern sanctuary
movement in the United States began during the Vietnam War. A
number of conscientious objectors who had been drafted sought
refuge from authorities in churches and chapels. Law enforcement officers went in to these spaces and dragged the young men
out. After a public outcry, the U.S. government created a policy regarding "sensitive locations," including houses of worship,
schools, and hospitals. Unless there are extraordinary circumstances, agents of the government will not enter these spaces to
remove people seeking shelter there.

Churches used this policy during the 1980s when a number
of refugees sought asylum in the United States from the wars
in Central America and the death squads those wars fostered.
Congregations around the country allowed asylum seekers to live
within the church property in order to impede their deportation.
Seeking sanctuary in a church is a last resort, generally only considered by people who have already received their final deportation orders.

While the sanctuary movement had been largely dormant
since the early 1990s, it experienced a rebirth in 2006 and again in
2014. A number of people have been given sanctuary at Southside
Presbyterian since Alison became pastor. One guest stayed only
28 days; another stayed 461.

A ministry of sanctuary requires the support of a whole community and involves all of the forms of ministry already discussed.
Alison's congregation is connected with communities vulnerable
to unjust deportation and involved with other efforts for justice.
Those who are given sanctuary partner with the congregation
to amplify the voices of those seeking asylum and publicize the
problems they face. Sheltering in the church impedes the officers
of Homeland Security so the community can advocate for a safe,
legal resolution. While a guest is at Southside, different members
of the congregation volunteer to stay in the church with them, so
the guest is accompanied around the clock.

For Alison and her congregation, impeding deportations by providing sanctuary is not the ideal form of allyship. It would be preferable to work in solidarity with those who are oppressed to change the structures that cause these difficulties. Southside Presbyterian works to do this. However, while systemic injustice still exists, sanctuary is a powerful means to impede its operations. Alison suspects the need for sanctuary will increase in the coming years and is hopeful that congregations will rise to the occasion. She reports that before November 2016, there were roughly 250 churches involved in the sanctuary movement. By February 2017, that number was approaching 700.

■ ■ ■

Celebrate

The final strategy we will cover here is celebration. Racism, heterosexism, and other forms of structural oppression devalue particular people and cultures. Celebrating those people and cultures is therefore an act of resistance. This is seen clearly in pride marches, which celebrate LGBTQ people and cultures and affirm their value.

Oppression functions, in part, by creating fear and despair. Celebration and joy are vital ways to reject and counter this functioning.

■ ■ ■

Marilyn's Story

When Marilyn McCord Adams was teaching at Yale Divinity School, there were members of the faculty and student body who interpreted Christianity in such a way that they rejected the legitimacy of same-sex love. LGBTQ students lived, ate, studied, and worshiped in a community where they were judged faulty by some of their peers and professors. They attended a school where the theological status of their experiences and identities was openly debated. In this context, Marilyn threw a dessert party every semester for LGBTQ students. She spent days baking elaborate cakes and cookies. Students were welcomed into her home, where they found a large table laden with goodies, an elaborate welcome, a safe community, and tangible affirmation of the love of God for LGBTQ people.

■   ■   ■

Another important role of celebration is that it strengthens bonds and friendships. When allies join a struggle and connect with people across racial and cultural divides, those relationships ought not be confined to political activism. Instead, they should flourish into the kind of loving relationships to which we are all called. This means we should not only share one another's struggles but also celebrate one another's joys. These relationships themselves are a form of resistance to the segregation that upholds racism and a glimmer of the right relationships to which we are called by God.

Finally, celebration sustains us in the struggle. It provides spiritual nourishment and concrete encouragement to those who are marginalized and to allies who will be criticized for their efforts. The struggle for justice is long, rough, and marked with setbacks. Many of the specific things we work for—like a policy reform or a wage increase—will never happen. To keep going, we need to remind ourselves that even our failures are worthwhile, because the community of struggle is an attempt to move toward the future to which we are called.

Allies will be criticized from all sides.

1. We will be condemned by those who explicitly or implicitly support the unjust systems we seek to change. Unfortunately,

some of these people will be friends, family, or colleagues that we did not expect to fall into this category.

2. We will also be challenged by the people with whom we ally ourselves. Often this will be because we need to learn more or make a mistake. However, sometimes when we step into relationship with oppressed communities, we simply will be the ones who hear the anger and frustration toward all members of the dominant culture. If someone is the only white person in a room, an honest conversation about the realities of systemic racism will hurt. Even if we try not to be defensive or take it personally, an honest appraisal of white supremacy and its ongoing legacy causes pain.

3. We will also be criticized by that section of society that thinks so very carefully about every possible form of activism that they find them all inadequate and decide the only morally pure way forward is complaint. In Ferguson, black protestors put their hands in the air and chanted, "Hands up! Don't shoot!" Some white people who intellectually reject racism found it offensive that white allies would also put their hands in the air and repeat this chant. They argued that this was dishonest, since white people are not in the same social location in regard to police officers. It is wise to be wary of arguments from those in the dominant culture that ultimately proclaim the moral superiority of inaction.

In the face of such criticism, it is important to remember why we started down this path. It is not for the approval of friends or family. It is not for the approval of people who are marginalized! Rather, is a faithful turning toward the call of God. It is a turning toward who we, ourselves, are called to be. When things are difficult, it is vital that we celebrate the new relationships and insights in our lives. And there will be a lot to celebrate! The strangest thing about struggling for justice—the hardest thing to explain—is the joy involved. The Spirit that draws us forward together is also the spirit of laughter and delight.

The various forms of ministry mentioned here (connect, amplify, advocate, accompany, impede, and celebrate) overlap and intermingle. While one form of action might be central at a given moment, the long-term struggle for justice involves all of them. The work of the water protectors at Standing Rock exemplifies the combination of these forms of action.

■ ■ ■

Rebecca's Story

The Dakota Access Pipeline (DAPL), owned by Energy Transfer Partners, L.P., is intended to transport massive quantities of crude oil. By building almost entirely on private land, the developers have avoided having to conduct an environmental impact statement that would detail potential ecological damage from the pipeline. They also failed to consult with the indigenous communities in the area. The proposed route of the pipeline would violate sites sacred to indigenous populations and endanger the water supply of the Standing Rock Reservation. Beginning in 2016, the Standing Rock Sioux tribe and others have engaged in daily activism to protect the water and the sacred sites. The water protectors have created temporary camps on the northern edge of the reservation, roughly 2.5 miles from the location where the pipeline would cross Lake Oahe in the Missouri River. A sacred fire has been tended at the Oceti Sakowin camp since August 2016, as water protectors have gathered to pray, to protest, and to prevent the completion of the DAPL.

Rev. Dr. Rebecca Voelkel, Director of the Center for Sustainable Justice, has visited the camps at Standing Rock as an ally three times. The first time was in September 2016, at the invitation of the Director of the Council of American Indian Ministries for the United Church of Christ. Rebecca describes the camps at Standing Rock as embodying each of the forms of ministry discussed above.

Standing Rock has become a place of great *connection*, as nearly three hundred different indigenous nations from around the world have sent official delegations to support the movement. Flags from these nations line the main road into the camps. In addition, allies from all over the United States and the world have been invited to participate at different moments. Notably, there are guiding principles of behavior for those who make the pilgrimage to Standing Rock, including recognizing indigenous leadership, no drugs, no violence, no unauthorized actions, and no property damage.

Rebecca revisited Standing Rock in November 2016, when the water protectors issued a call for clergy members of all faiths to participate. Over five hundred clergy went to the camp to participate in a ceremonial repudiation of the Doctrine of Discovery, a series of papal decrees that became woven into U.S. law, which supported the theft of land from indigenous communities and the killing of non-Christian persons when deemed "necessary." During a ritual, seven tribal elders stood at the sacred fire as representatives from Christian denominations that had taken official action to reject the doctrine read statements of repentance and repudiation. A symbolic copy of the Doctrine of Discover was presented to the elders, who took embers from the fire to burn it.

The work of the water protectors has shone a spotlight on the DAPL and the environmental harm it promises. The pipeline, completed mostly on private land, had received very little media attention or public scrutiny before the creation of the camps and the activism of the water protectors. The concerns of the indigenous communities have been *amplified* by the media attention garnered by the water protectors. This has involved a significant amount of education regarding the histories of the Lakota,

Dakota, Nakota, and other nations; the legal history of broken treaties with the United States; the sacred stories, beliefs, and practices of indigenous communities; and the ecological realities of running crude oil under the Missouri River.

The *advocacy* of the water protectors is clear: they demand that the DAPL not be completed on the planned route. They have lobbied local, regional, and national governmental agencies as well as waging lawsuits. Everyone who visits the camps at Standing Rock is asked and expected to participate in local advocacy when they return home. In response to such advocacy, the city council in Rebecca's hometown of Minneapolis passed a resolution condemning the DAPL.

While allies have played a role of *accompaniment* throughout the protest, the clearest example occurred in December. The Army Corps of Engineers and the governor of North Dakota announced the camps would be cleared on December 5, 2016. Given that militarized police had already used tear gas, rubber bullets, water cannons, and percussion grenades against the protesters, the evacuation order carried the threat of force. Leaders at Standing Rock asked for allies to come and accompany the water protectors. Over two thousand U.S. veterans arrived. Federal authorities halted construction on the pipeline. In addition, tribal elders and veterans participated in a forgiveness ceremony, in which the veterans were given an opportunity to repent for military actions against indigenous communities throughout U.S. history, to accompany their repentance with acts of repair, and to receive forgiveness.

The veterans who arrived in Standing Rock accompanied the water protectors and *impeded* the planned unjust action of clearing the camp. The images of protestors being drenched by water cannons in freezing temperatures were already in the news. What would it look like to have police shooting rubber bullets at U.S. veterans? Here the activities of connection, amplification, accompaniment, and impeding intertwine. In ways both symbolic and concrete, the water protectors of Standing Rock were actively impeding the construction of the pipeline. This included the advocacy work and amplification of the issues, but it also included concrete acts such as water protectors chaining themselves to equipment to impede the destruction of burial grounds.

Ceremony and prayer were built into every activity in the camps. While the catalyst for the gathering at Standing Rock was the DAPL, there was tremendous emphasis on building sacred community and *celebrating* the indigenous communities participating. This celebration was a sacred cultural reclamation that imbued the entire movement. Rebecca recalled that during her first visit, there was a microphone set up by the sacred fire. Different elders would stand to speak and educate those gathered about the history of his or her community. A Lakota elder started a traditional song. She asked those who knew it to join her and explained to those who were unfamiliar with the language that the words translated "We are alive." In the midst of a long history of oppression, to sing "We are alive" was a powerful celebration of Lakota identity, resilience, and strength.

The ritual aspects of Standing Rock testify to the profound strength of activism that is not merely religiously grounded but also imbued with spirituality throughout. The ceremonies involving clergy repudiating the doctrine of discovery and veterans seeking forgiveness were immensely powerful in acknowledging injustice, recognizing trauma, and opening toward healing. Another activist who has visited Standing Rock, Dr. Marion Grau, writes that the entire camp is itself "a ceremony, a call to bring forth the best in each of us, and to act accordingly."[8] Rebecca states, "I am amazed by the spiritual fortitude of indigenous people at Standing Rock to invite white allies—especially white Christian allies, given the particular harms done by Christians—to be part of this struggle for justice."

■ ■ ■

THE STRUGGLE CONTINUES

That tricky question of how to first engage the struggle for justice will soon seem like the distant past. Once we connect to this work, opportunities arise at every turn. Soon the question will not be how to get started but how to set limits so we don't burn out from exhaustion. While the contribution of each person is deeply important, no one person can do all that is needed. At this point, it might be worthwhile to remember the earlier activity, with sections for abilities, assets, and access. The exercise is intended to help new allies identify a variety of ways in which they could participate in the struggle. In particular, it aims to steer people away from seeing only their top-level abilities, assets, or access points as the primary ways to contribute. However, once you get more involved and the question is not how to start but how to limit, the exercise can be used in the opposite way: prioritize activities that require your top-level skills. It makes sense for a lawyer who can also cook to first connect with a group by cooking. Once she has learned more and been engaged, it might make sense to leave the cooking to someone else in favor of using her legal expertise. Rev. Alison Harrington advises, "Get in where you fit in!"

DISCUSSION QUESTIONS

1. If you were to do the exercise described at the beginning of this chapter, what would you list as your abilities? Your assets? Your access?

2. What concrete opportunities to work for justice and healing have your connections and contacts opened to you?

3. Have you ever contacted your state or federal representatives

in order to advocate for a policy or cause? What did you learn that you would share with others just getting started?

4. Can you name times in your life when, working for a more just society, you experienced the joy and celebration the authors describe?

CHAPTER FIVE

Examples to Follow

At various points in this book, we have discussed the problems with whiteness and the reasons why claiming whiteness as our primary identity continues the trajectory of racism. We've also mentioned a few strategies for identifying in different ways (e.g., by ethnicity or region—e.g., Italian or Appalachian). Another important element of identity is religion. Baptized Christians claim an identity secured by Jesus—we are members of the body of Christ.[1]

We also aspire to the identity of "allies." This is not a name we can simply claim for ourselves. Rather, the claim to being an ally is one that we make with our lives. When we live in ways that foster right relationships, when we struggle against injustice, and when we use our resources to promote the flourishing of all, we enact an identity as allies.

When we do this we are not alone and not without guides. Throughout the long history of racism and heterosexism, there have always been at least a few members of dominant cultures who allied themselves with marginalized people in order to work for justice. Our hope is to emulate these courageous people and, in so doing, to place ourselves in their company. Here are some examples of allies—of straight people and white people who lived out a different identity. We hope to claim these brave souls as our foremothers and forefathers in the struggle.

MYLES HORTON

> "I think if I had to put a finger on what I consider a good education, a good radical education, it wouldn't be anything about methods or techniques. It would be about loving people first."[2]

Learning to be in right relationships across societal borders was central to Myles Horton's educational vision and to the Highlander Folk School, which he founded. In the fall of 1959, the state of Tennessee revoked the charter of the Highlander Folk School. Deputy sheriffs arrested the students of different races who were studying citizenship and padlocked the gates on the grounds. The school and its students were violating Tennessee laws that prohibited their learning together. In response, Horton quipped: "You can padlock a building, you can't padlock an idea."[3]

Myles Horton was born poor and white on July 9, 1905, in rural Tennessee. His parents had been schoolteachers who lost their positions when the educational requirements for teachers were increased. As a child, Horton's parents worked in factories and as sharecroppers. His father also joined the Workers Alliance union. As a young teen, Horton moved out of his parents' home in order to attend the regional high school. He supported himself during this time by working at a sawmill and then a box factory where he witnessed the bosses taunt and speak down to his coworkers. He helped form a union at the factory, which successfully agitated for a pay raise.[4]

While studying education at Cumberland College in Tennessee, Horton taught summer Bible classes to impoverished white people from the mountains. He learned about poverty and exploitation from his students as they shared with him stories of being swindled out of their families' land, and sometimes their homes as well, by fast-talking representatives of logging and coal companies. After college, Horton attended Union Theological Seminary in New York City. "As his studies at Union continued, Horton developed an idea for a school that would teach the crafts and wisdom of the Appalachian People while empowering them to stand against the greed and tyranny of the corporate establishment that was taking advantage of the people."[5]

At this same time, Horton met two ministers from Denmark who told him that his idea for a school was similar to that of the Danish Folk schools that focused on learning from experience. Horton traveled to Denmark in 1931 to learn about these schools. Horton left Denmark with the epiphany that "You can go to school all your life, you'll never figure it out because you are trying to get an answer that can only come from the people in the life situation."[6] Central to Horton's pedagogy was the belief that we all have something to learn from each other—that we are all teachers and we are all students—and we learn best together. Musing in his journal about what would become of the Highlander Folk School, Horton reflected, "The school will be for young men and women of the mountains and workers from the factories. Negroes would be among the students who will live in close personal contact with teachers. Out of their experiential learning through living, working, and studying together could come an understanding of how to take their place intelligently in the changing world."[7]

In 1932, Horton founded the Southern Mountains School, which was soon renamed the Highlander Folk school, on donated land in Monteagle, Tennessee. Highlander focused on labor issues at first and received support from the Committee for Industrial Organization (the CIO that was later absorbed into the AFL-CIO). At this time, unions routinely excluded black people from joining, which worked to benefit the owners of the textile mills and coal mines that used black people as scabs (nonunion workers willing to take over the jobs of union members on strike). Horton recognized that while racial segregation primarily hurt black people, it also hurt poor and working-class white people. By the 1940s, Highlander was offering classes on civil rights that were attended by both black and white working people from Appalachia and the South.

By the 1950s, Highlander had become an incubator of what would become the civil rights movement. Civil rights workers including Martin Luther King Jr., Rosa Parks, Fannie Lou Hamer, Andrew Young, and Septima Clark spoke, facilitated, and otherwise participated in workshops and classes at Highlander. The students they taught would soon be marching in Selma, boycotting busses in Montgomery, and sitting at lunch counters in Nashville. History books report that Rosa Parks was a student at Highlander. She was also a teacher, sharing her experiences with the white students. Parks said,

> My life has been hard. As a small girl I had to run—or thought I had—from the Ku Klux Klan to escape being killed. My father was cheated out of his land by a white man. I did not get much of an education. I could not register to vote. . . . I did attend a workshop at the Highlander School, and I want to tell you that the only reason I don't hate every white man alive is Highlander and Myles Horton.[8]

A vital component of Highlander's early civil rights work in the 1950s was teaching impoverished black people how to read and write. High rates of illiteracy in the black community were the legacy of earlier laws that made it illegal to *teach* black people how to read and write as well as for Black people to *learn* how to read and write. Literacy in the black community was also depressed due to vastly inferior, underfunded, and segregated schools. It has been claimed that Highlander's Citizenship Schools were "the largest and clearly the most effective mass literacy campaign ever undertaken in the United States—successful largely because the campaign was not about literacy, but about the right to participate in a democratic society."[9]

After the Highlander was padlocked and seized by the state in 1959, the buildings were burned to the ground. Horton began offering its citizenship classes out of the offices of the Southern Christian Leadership Conference—the preeminent civil rights organization of the time made famous by Martin Luther King Jr.'s words and Ella Baker's works. In 1961, a new generation of civil rights activists began arriving at Highlander. These activists, including Bob Moses, would form the Student Nonviolent Coordinating Committee (SNCC) with the facilitation and guidance of Ella Baker and other Highlander alumni. SNCC and a relaunched Highlander Research and Education Center started voter registration drives, sit-in demonstrations, and Freedom Schools that formed a significant part of what is recalled as the civil rights movement.

With his life and through his work at the Highlander school, Horton avoided speaking for black people and never asserted that he taught black people anything.

> The thing about Highlander was that the real answers never came from Highlander, but from the activists themselves who went there. At the end of their training session under Horton, the SNCC activists devised their own plans for entering into and mobilizing communities in the Magnolia State [MS]. The style and success of the organizing was their own, but it didn't come from out of nowhere. It was informed by their encounter with organizing methods like Horton's. Without such methods, communities would have been led by SNCC, instead of leading the way themselves.[10]

The SNCC Legacy Project and Duke University wrote about

Mr. Horton and Highlander: "education wasn't exclusively about giving information to people, but also about discovering a perspective with them. This would greatly influence SNCC's approach to organizing."[11] This mindset is crucial to work for justice, especially on the part of those who seek to be allies to oppressed communities in the struggle for liberation.

Myles Horton, who died on January 19, 1990, has been hailed by Dr. Cornel West as "an indescribably courageous and visionary white brother. . . ."[12] Through the Highlander Folk School and the Highlander Education and Resource Center, Horton forged a model for social change that synthesized his nontraditional understanding of education with his observations on the power of organized people. His work was informed by his personal experiences with poverty and injustice and by his mother's insistence that "God is love and therefore you love your neighbors."[13]

A vision of loving and mutual relationships across divides of race and class was foundational to Horton's work. This vision set the goal of Horton's efforts and also the method—preventing those from the dominant culture from repeating oppressive patterns. Allies often falter when we are focused tightly on a particular political goal or social outcome. We are tempted to sidestep the hard work of mutual relationships in order to be more immediately effective or efficient. Horton prioritized loving relationships, and loving relationships curtail such temptations.

To learn more about the Highlander Research and Education Center, visit their website: http://highlandercenter.org/.

ANNE BRADEN

"An older, African American leader that I respected highly told me I had to make a choice: be a part of the world of the lynchers or join the Other America—of people from the very beginning of this country who

> opposed injustice, and especially opposed racism and
> slavery. [He told me] I could be a part of that—that it
> existed today and offered me a home to live in. I felt
> like, well, that's what I wanna be a part of."[14]

Not long ago, white people who were friendly with black people were reviled, and those who participated in the struggle for racial justice were labeled "race traitors." Anne Braden and her husband, Carl, were two of the few white Americans who were formally charged with sedition for their solidarity in the struggle with black people for racial justice. Carl Braden was convicted and sentenced to fifteen years in prison, though his conviction was later overturned. Anne Braden was never tried in court, but she and her husband were repeatedly tried by the white press and ostracized by the white community of Louisville, Kentucky, where they lived. The specific "offense" that led to their sedition charge was their purchase and transfer of a home in a white Louisville neighborhood in 1954. Andrew and Charlotte Wade, black friends of the Bradens, were unable to buy a house in this particular neighborhood because no realtor would facilitate the sale. The Bradens bought the house on the Wades' behalf in order to circumvent this discrimination. When the white neighbors realized what had taken place, they burned a cross on the lawn, shot out the windows, and threw dynamite at the house. The Wades were never able to move in. The Bradens were charged with sedition under the presumption that they had to be Communists to do such a thing. No one was ever prosecuted for the violence perpetrated against the Wades and Bradens.[15]

Anne McCarty Braden was born middle-class and white on July 28, 1924, in Louisville, Kentucky, to parents who "fully embraced the norms of Southern racial hierarchy."[16] Braden lived throughout the South as a child and studied literature and journalism at Stratford Junior College and Randolph-Macon Women's College in Virginia before moving to Birmingham to report for local newspapers in 1945. Through her work as a journalist covering the Birmingham court, Ms. Braden saw two unequal standards of justice at work: one white, one black. In "A Letter to White Southern Women," published in 1972, she recounted covering a case of a black man who was sentenced to twenty years in prison for "assault with intent to ravish." A poor, white woman had accused the defendant of looking at her from across a country road in an "insulting" way. Braden recalls this story as the incident that first made her "aware" that "no white woman reared in the South—or perhaps anywhere in this racist country—can find freedom as a woman until she deals in her own consciousness with the question of race." Ms. Braden registered her dismay with the prosecutor in the case but did little else.

> At the time, I wondered how that woman could do this cruel thing to the black man—sending him to prison for 20 years for absolutely nothing. It was only later that I realized the horror of what she was doing to herself. Tomorrow, after her day as a queen, she would go back to a life of poverty and boredom: waiting on her father, on her brothers, and someday on a husband—paying with a lifetime of drudgery for those magic moments when she could achieve the status of a wronged white woman. It was even longer before I realized that my conflicts that day also arose from questions about myself—before I came to understand that my position and that of the woman on the witness stand were not very different after all.[17]

As a twenty-two-year-old journalist, Braden had considered herself a free and liberated woman. Yet after her protestations to the prosecutor were ignored, and she herself did nothing more regarding the case, Braden's image of herself changed. She later wrote, "sitting that day in the prosecutor's office, I was just one more brainless woman. By my acquiescence, I was part of the conspiracy that said white women must be protected."[18]

In 1947, Ms. Braden returned to Kentucky and began reporting for the *Louisville Times*, covering the early stirrings of the emerging civil rights movement. She also researched the history of white women in the South. She learned about the leading role of white women in the abolition movement at a time when they were not allowed to vote and largely proscribed from acting in public. She also learned more about the lynching of black men, often by white mobs self-charged with the "duty" to restore the "honor" of white women who had allegedly been raped or otherwise dishonored by black boys and men. She learned "how rape had been made a capital crime only after the Civil War, after Reconstruction brought poor whites and blacks in the South together to create a better society. It was then that those who formerly ruled had to institute a new terror to come back to power."[19] Braden describes the "turning point in her life" coming when she got involved in the case of Mr. Willie McGee, a black man sentenced to death for the rape of a white woman in 1945. Mr. McGee was executed by the state of Mississippi in 1951, despite protests of white women organized by Ms. Braden, who were no longer willing to, "be used as things, as tools of white supremacy."[20]

At one point, Braden led a delegation of white women to the state capital in Jackson to lobby the governor. The group was detained by Jackson police and put in "protective custody." "They put us in a jail cell. It struck me as symbolic of what the South's protection of its white women really means."[21] Braden wrote how the local police berated the women as foolish and ignorant "Yankees" and how one officer became so angry he had to be restrained by other officers when Braden revealed that she was a Southerner and thus a "traitor."

> In a single moment of action, I had placed myself on the "other side"—the other side from that cop who at first wanted to protect me, and when I didn't want to be protected, wanted to kill me . . . the other side from the prosecutor who took my brain and my

humanity away from me by granting me favors as a young reporter because I was an attractive woman . . . the other side from the people in Mississippi who were determined to kill Willie McGee, who had made his accuser a heroine for a time, and used her for all of her life . . . the other side from the people I had grown up with, who had taught me so carefully where a woman's place was . . . the other side from the rulers of the South who treated black people like children and put white women on pedestals—and turned on both in fury when they asserted their humanity. . . .

I was on the other side from the death and decay that gripped the society I lived in. For in an exploitive society, there are always two sides. And at some point, one must choose.[22]

Braden lays bare the ways in which racism and sexism pitted white women and black men (and women) against each other and white workers against black workers. This prevented alliances based on shared, if different, experiences of oppression that might otherwise undermine sexism, racism, and worker exploitation.

Braden both taught and studied at the Highlander School with Ella Baker and other SNCC activists in the 1950s and 60s. In addition to her writing, Braden was actively involved with the efforts of SNCC in the 1960s, including the Open Housing movement in Louisville in the late 1960s, the school desegregation struggle of the 1970s, the efforts of Jesse Jackson and the Rainbow Coalition in the 1980s, and—later in life—efforts to fight environmental racism, oppose police brutality, and end mass incarceration. Braden focused her influence on white people; she and her husband traveled through the Deep South in the 50s and 60s seeking white allies to the civil rights movement. Unlike many white people both then and now, Braden understood the Black Power movement as a growing consciousness of self-determination on the part of black activists who rightly bristled at the paternalism of many white allies. Braden was a powerful mentor to a generation of young white activists.

Braden was declared "the most amazing white woman"[23] by Rev. Martin Luther King Jr. in 1957. Angela Davis said that Braden's efforts "enabled vast and often spectacular social changes . . . that most of her contemporaries during the 1950s would never have been able to imagine."[24] And the Rev. Jesse Jackson wrote, "When the civil rights struggle engulfed the South, Anne Braden was one of the courageous few who crossed the color line to fight for racial justice. Her history is a proud and fascinating one . . . Anne Braden is indeed a 'subversive southerner. . . .'"[25]

When the dominant order of the day is one of injustice, the only just thing to do is to be subversive. Anne Braden died in Louisville on March 6, 2006, after a long life of subverting injustice.

There are two ways that Braden's example is particularly important for allies today. First, Braden had a profound grasp of intersectionality. She saw the ways that racism and sexism interact and rely on one another. Second, although Braden had been raised as a white woman, she chose to claim as her primary identity not her whiteness but her resistance to oppression and her solidarity with those seeking justice. For Braden, this choice did not signify a loss of status or privilege (although she did lose those) but rather a step away from the "death and decay" of systemic injustice.

To learn more, visit the website of the Anne Braden Institute for Social Justice Research at the University of Louisville: http://louisville.edu/braden.

JEANNE MANFORD

"There is a lot of talk about gays and lesbians these days. But in everything we say and do, particularly for Christians, love must come first. And not the love that condemns first, or judges first, or labels first. But the love that loves first. Because God is love."[26]

These words were written by Fr. James Martin the day after Jeanne Manford died. He wrote, "she loved prophetically. That is, she publicly expressed her love for a group of marginalized people before it was safe to do so."[27] Manford did this by proclaiming to the world, in a letter to the editor of the *New York Post* that was published on April 29, 1972: "I have a homosexual son and I love him."[28] At that time, homosexuality was still listed as a mental illness in the *Diagnostic and Statistical Manual of Mental Disorders* (DSM), sex between men was still a criminal act, and gay people were vocally condemned by many Christians.[29]

Jeanne Manford was born into a middle-class white family on December 4, 1920, in Queens, New York. She briefly went to college in Alabama but returned to New York after her father died suddenly. Manford enrolled in Queens College in her thirties, obtained a bachelor degree, and became a schoolteacher. She married and had three children: Charles, Morty, and Suzanne. In 1966, Charles overdosed and died while away at school.[30]

Her son Morty was an openly gay and politically active man. On April 15, 1972, Morty was severely beaten while handing out leaflets with the Gay Activists Alliance inside the fiftieth annual Inner Circle dinner in New York City. The Inner Circle dinner is a big name event attended by local and national political figures. Morty's beating was witnessed by several NYC police officers who did not stop it. Though his assailant was arrested, there was little outcry about the incident. Jeanne Manford was righteously outraged by her son's beating, the complicity of those witnesses who did nothing, and the nonplussed response of the press. By all accounts, her outrage was heightened by the memory of having outlived one son. When she received a call from NYPD informing her of Morty's beating, she took action. Suzanne Manford recalled: "My mother was beside herself with rage that anybody could hurt her child. She'd already lost one, and the fact that she could have lost another . . . she was seething."[31] Manford's first act was to call the *New York Post* and demand reporting on the assault. When that failed, she sent a letter to the editor to proclaim what should have been obvious: She loved her son. His being gay was hardly a reason not to love him. Nonetheless, her public proclamation was unprecedented. In 1972, the heterosexism of our society was so great that the stigma shamed families with LGBTQ children; these families often lived in fear that their child's sexual orientation might be used to halt a career, lose friends, or ostracize them from a church community.

On June 25, 1972, Manford marched beside her son in the Christopher Street Liberation Day March, the precursor to New York City's Gay Pride Parade, holding a sign that read, "Parents of Gays: Unite in Support of Our Children." Her message elicited enthusiastic cheers along the way, which she mistakenly thought were directed at Dr. Benjamin Spock who was marching just behind her. After the parade, marchers sought her out to ask if she might speak with their parents. In the ensuing weeks and months, she received calls at home from other parents of LGBTQ children who were seeking support and understanding. With this obvious need for support and advocacy, Jeanne Manford and her husband, Jules, founded Parents of Gays (POG) on March 11, 1973. Only twenty people attended the first meeting, held at a Methodist church in the lower west side of Manhattan. POG was a "safe place for parents to come together to learn to get over their own upsets and confusions about their children's sexual orientation and to learn to accept them as they were."[32]

By 1979, POG groups had formed across the United States. Representatives met in Washington, DC, after the National March for Gay and Lesbian Rights to form Parents and Friends of Lesbians and Gays (PFLAG). PFLAG became a clearinghouse for information and advocacy materials. It became a well-known group after the beloved advice columnist Dear Abby repeatedly referred scared gay teens and confused straight parents to PFLAG in her nationally syndicated newspaper column.[33]

PFLAG has become a leading player in the liberation struggle of the LGBTQ community. Today PFLAG lists as their priorities: "Proud People, Loving Families, Safe Communities, and a Diverse & Inclusive World."[34] They work for a world where LGBTQ people are freed from the shame imposed by a heterosexist society and can be proud of who they are; they work to support the families and friends of LGBT people in their efforts toward LGBTQ equality; they support initiatives to protect LGBTQ people from violence and discrimination; and they work "to create a world where difference is celebrated, and all people are valued inclusive of their sexual orientation, gender identity, and gender expression."[35] One of PFLAG's signature efforts is their "Cultivating Respect: Safe Schools for All" initiative that works to combat heterosexism and the bullying of LGBTQ children in schools.

Manford's efforts to love and protect her son provide us with several crucial lessons. First and foremost, she shows the power of love. Manford acted because she loved her son. Despite living in a society that loathed, feared, rejected, and judged LGBTQ people, her love for her son inoculated her from the forces that conditioned others to hate LGBTQ people.

"She was just a mom, walking with her son in a parade," said Terry DeCrescenzo, a longtime advocate for gay and lesbian teens in Los Angeles. "That was what made her so compelling. She was simply standing with her son, bearing witness to the truth of his life."[36] To bear witness is to act publicly with knowledge, particularly when injustice is observed. Manford bore witness by publicly proclaiming that she loved her son and that all LGBTQ people are children who ought to be loved by their families and protected by their society. *Social* justice by definition is achieved via *public* struggle.

Social justice is not achieved via the efforts of Wonder Women or Supermen but rather through the organized efforts of ordinary people who believe a better world is possible and are committed to making it so. Manford had little power acting alone, but when she founded POG/PFLAG she was able to work with thousands of families across the land to change attitudes, policies, and laws. Organization works to amplify one's message, it harnesses various skills that no one individual possesses, it pools resources of time and money, and it influences elections. Manford acted publicly and with others for justice.

Manford is a model activist, sometimes described as the mother of the Gay/Straight ally movement, because she didn't speak for her son or for gay people. She spoke from her place as the mother of a gay son. She worked with friends and families of LGBTQ people to break their silence and end their unwitting complicity with the persecution of their loved ones by organizing publicly for equal justice. Jeanne Manford died on January 8, 2013.[37]

KATRINA BROWNE

"Traveling the country while making a film, I've been struck by the fact that the vast majority of white Americans do not consider themselves 'racist.' In the North, we especially presume ourselves innocent. I certainly did."[38]

Katrina Browne thought of herself as innocent, despite knowing that she was a direct descendant of the largest slave trading family in American history. Black activists for racial justice often use the expression "get woke" to indicate becoming more aware of structural inequality. White people often stay in a state of somnolent amnesia, where we forget what we know of racism and its history. Any consciousness we have of it seems distant, muted, and void of emotion. Katrina Browne was still in that state, to some degree, in 1992.

As an upper-middle-class white woman and recent college graduate, Browne cofounded the organization Public Allies at the age of twenty-five. Public Allies seeks, "to create a just and equitable society and the diverse leadership to sustain it."[39] They do so by partnering with nonprofit organizations where "allies" from the community that is served by the nonprofit are placed in, "paid full-time nonprofit apprenticeships and rigorous training." Public Allies participants are representative of the racial and ethnic diversity of our society, so the apprenticeships and training provide a platform for cross-racial and cross-ethnic relationships to develop at a young age in a setting of mutual respect.[40]

However, it was not until Browne, by then a seminary student, received a note from her grandmother in 1995 that she became acutely aware of racial issues. The note was a brief history of Ms. Browne's family, the De Wolfs, which contained a passing mention that the family business was slave trading. "I had a double shock. First that I was descended from slave traders, and the second was that I realized already knew. It gave me a sense of total disbelief, this feeling of shame that I had buried it. I subsequently talked to my college roommate who said, 'you talked about this in college,' and I said, 'I did? I have no memory of that.'"[41]

Browne's prior knowledge of her family's past had been shaped by the history she was taught in school. History is written by the victors.[42] Documents preserved by the American Historical Society and readily available for online research describe the De Wolfs as, "ever patriotic and true, offering themselves without reservation to the causes of liberty and justice." They are remembered as a family of politicians, priests, bishops, and philanthropists whose wealth came from their, "splendid capacity for business enterprise, [which] they developed [into] a mercantile and shipping industry of large proportions."[43] Nowhere is it mentioned that their business was buying and selling more than ten thousand people kidnapped from Africa. Such skewed and incomplete historical accounts form the consciousness of white America—our public memory.

Browne decided to explore her family history further. She

wrote to two hundred direct descendants of the DeWolfs and invited them to learn more about their family's legacy by retracing the steps of the people kidnapped by their ancestors. The vehicle for this project was a documentary film, *Traces of the Trade: A Story from the Deep North*. Brown and nine other family members began their journey at the family homestead, Linden Place, a mansion in Bristol, Rhode Island, that is now a museum. They traveled to the dungeon in Ghana where enslaved African people were herded like cattle before being shipped. They traveled to the plantations in Cuba where enslaved African people worked while the DeWolfs waited for their resale value to rise. And they traveled to the auction block where human beings were stripped of their humanity and sold. Along the way, they learned from historians about the true involvement of the North, and the entire United States, in the slave trade.[44]

Slavery was not perpetrated solely by those wealthy families that owned enslaved Africans; everyone in America was implicated to some extent. In Bristol, Rhode Island; New London, Connecticut; Boston, Massachusetts; and elsewhere, the labor of slaves and the economy of slavery employed carpenters who built the slave ships, coopers who built the barrels to transport slave produced rum and gin, and smiths who produced manacles and shackles, among other trades. In Lawrence, Massachusetts and Lowell, Massachusetts, textile mills spun cotton picked by slaves, creating fabric that clothed America and harnessed the wind of slave ships. In Hartford, Connecticut, insurance companies such as Aetna insured slaves—not in the sense of providing them health insurance but in the sense of protecting their owners' assets. In New York, shares in slave holding companies and slave ships were sold to ordinary white people across the land. Slave-generated wealth built churches; funded charitable endowments; endowed colleges; purchased businesses not directly linked with the slave trade; financed mayoral, congressional, senatorial, gubernatorial, *and* presidential campaigns. In fact, the DeWolf family invested in Thomas Jefferson's campaign. In turn, a family member was appointed the Customs Inspector for the Bristol port, which enabled the DeWolf family to continue importing enslaved Africans after federal law had banned the transatlantic slave trade. When slavery finally came to an end in America, the political power bought with slave-produced wealth did not disappear but continued to function in the interests of white supremacy.

Browne urges concerned white people to do "white work" in white spaces; to meet with other white people to learn this history and feel the subsequent emotions in a space that does not burden black people with the responsibility for teaching us or consoling us. But of course this is just a starting point. Browne suggests that white people seeking racial justice can engage in some of the following activities:

- Form a task force in your religious congregation, school, civic group, workplace, or fraternal order to uncover the organization's historic relationship to slavery, and/or form an antiracism committee
- Research your local history of slavery/slave trade and ancillary businesses.
- Engage a particular school you are connected to, your local school district, and/or text book companies in a dialogue about how to teach the history of the slave trade/slavery in ways that include the role of the North as well as the South and which describe the centrality of slavery for the political, economic, and social development of the U.S.
- Learn more about the legacy of slavery today and take public action.
- Learn about legislative proposals.
- Communities of faith can engage on many levels, including via sermons, creating liturgies/rituals of atonement and reconciliation, getting involved in your local community, partnering with a congregation with members of a different

racial group, advocating for resolutions in your larger church body, and for legislation.

- Create a book discussion group.
- Expand your experience.
- Research connections between Native American history, Latino history, and Asian American history and the history of African slavery and its aftermath.
- Gather your family at the dinner table and have a discussion about family history and the history of race in the U.S.
- How could you celebrate July 4th differently? In 1852 Frederick Douglas delivered a famous speech in which he said: "This Fourth of July is yours, not mine. You may rejoice, I must mourn."[45] How can we reflect on the good and bad of our history and learn from it all?
- Support the campaign to end modern slavery.[46]

With these suggestions, Browne offers white Americans an avenue to avoid continuing the "mundane complicity of ordinary people—church going people"[47] of Bristol, Rhode Island, and "Everytown," USA, that quietly benefitted from the exploitation and oppression of African Americans. Browne calls us to engage in "civic love . . . an extension of the biblical call to love one's neighbor as oneself. It [is a] definition of patriotism: a love of self that extended to love of fellow citizen, all of which created a national glue of commitment to the public good."[48] Civic love, a love which would address the systemic and structural injustices of our land, is the steadfast practice of democracy and the faithful practice of Christianity.

Browne's willingness to face the facts of history and their continuing implications is an example of repentance that enables allies to turn again toward love of God and neighbor. Through her research and travels, Browne learned that she is not innocent. However, neither is she guilty. Instead, she is a beloved child of

God, living in a broken world, who has found grace enough to turn toward a better future.

To learn more about Public Allies, visit their website: http:// publicallies.org/.

To learn more about the film *Traces of the Trade*, visit http:// www.tracesofthetrade.org/.

To learn more about Katrina Browne's current work, visit The Tracing Center at http://www.tracingcenter.org/.

DISCUSSION QUESTIONS

1. When the dominant culture tells the story of the struggle for justice, it makes members of that culture the heroes. What can we learn from the example of Myles Horton, Anne Braden, and Jeanne Manford about how to place our work as allies in the proper perspective?

2. The people profiled were ordinary people who changed our society. Change doesn't take place because superheroes fly in to rescue us. Superman and Wonder Woman are not real; ordinary people like Anne Braden and Jeanne Manford are. What can an ordinary person like yourself do to work for justice?

An Invitation

This book ends not with a conclusion but with an invitation. White supremacy, like any social system, is created and sustained by human actions. We can choose to create new systems as we work with movements for LGBTQ and racial equality.

This will involve building new relationships across social boundaries. We can choose to live in racially diverse neighborhoods and create racially diverse schools. We can choose to join bowling leagues, fishing groups, book clubs, and prayer partnerships that will introduce us to people from communities we might not otherwise meet. We can choose to broaden our circles of contacts, acquaintances, and—eventually—friends so that loving our neighbor might become a little bit easier.

It will also involve changing laws and policies. We can advocate for change on every level of government, from the school board to the White House, from local zoning laws to national budget allocations. We can choose to demonstrate, protest, educate ourselves and others, and provide concrete support for social justice organizations.

Being an ally is compassionate solidarity in action. Becoming an ally requires two leaps of faith. First, we believe that the world that God intends for us—a world of right relationships—will be better for each and every one of us. Justice benefits everybody. Loving God and neighbor will bring far more joy than the spoils of white supremacy. Second, we believe that each and all of us are beloved children of God who are invited to be part of what God is doing in the world. Together, we can move toward the future that God intends.

Notes

Foreword
1. Nelson Mandela, *Long Walk to Freedom: The Autobiography of Nelson Mandela*, 1st ed. (Boston: Little, Brown, 1994.

Introduction
1. WIS 10 News Staff, "FBI to Lead Investigation of Violent Incident at Spring Valley High School," WIS 10 (Columbia, SC), Nov. 19, 2016. http://www.wistv.com/story/30353999/sheriff-contacts-fbi-doj-to -investigate-violent-incident-involving-deputy-at-spring-valley-high -school.
2. In Susan Ratcliffe, ed., *Oxford Essential Quotations*, 3rd ed., http://www .oxfordreference.com/view/10.1093/acref/9780191804144.001.0001/q -oro-ed3-00016497.
3. Martin Luther King Jr., *Why We Can't Wait* (New York: Penguin, 1963), 74.
4. The following analysis is informed by Allan G. Johnson, *The Gender Knot: Unraveling Our Patriarchal Legacy* (Philadelphia: Temple University Press, 1997), 5. Johnson defines patriarchy as a social system operating in society that is "male dominated, male identified, and male centered," which functions to privilege masculinity and not simply a society where there are male chauvinists.
5. See Johnson, *The Gender Knot*, 5.
6. Martin V. Melose, "Automobile in American Life and Society," http://www .autolife.umd.umich.edu/Environment/E_Casestudy/E_casestudy.htm.

7. "Transportation Secretary Anthony Foxx on the Legacy of the U.S. Highway System," The Diane Rehm Show, http://thedianerehmshow .org/shows/2016-03-31/transportation-secretary-anthony-foxx-on -transportation-opportunity-and-the-legacy-of-the-u-s-highway-system.

8. See: Peggy McIntosh, *White Privilege and Male Privilege: A Personal Account of Coming to See Correspondences through Work in Women's Studies* (Wellesley, MA: Wellesley College, Center for Research on Women, 1988).

9. Bim Adewunmi, "Kimberlé Crenshaw on Intersectionality: 'I Wanted to Come Up with an Everyday Metaphor That Anyone Could Use,'" *New Statesman*, April 2, 2014, http://www.newstatesman.com/lifestyle/2014/04 /kimberl-crenshaw-intersectionality-i-wanted-come-everyday-metaphor -anyone-could.

10. See Sojourner Truth's "Ain't I a Woman: Sojourner Truth," National Parks Service, https://www.nps.gov/wori/learn/historyculture/sojourner-truth .htm.

11. The examples in these paragraphs are intentionally male and female. Theologian Judith Plaskow argues persuasively that the sin of pride is more aligned with traits and roles aligned to men, whereas women are more encouraged to be self-abnegating. In this way, chastising women not to be proud can amount to reinforcing sexist oppression. This is not always the case, but it merits attention. See Judith Plaskow, *Sex, Sin and Grace: Women's Experience and the Theologies of Reinhold Niebuhr and Paul Tillich* (New York: University Press of America, 1980).

12. Howard Thurman, *Jesus and the Disinherited* (Boston, MA: Beacon Press, 1976), 50, 27–28, 53.

13. Sally Kohn, "This Is What White People Can Do to Support #blacklivesmatter," *The Washington Post*, August 6, 2015, https://www .washingtonpost.com/posteverything/wp/2015/08/06/this-is-what-white -people-can-do-to-support-blacklivesmatter/?utm_term=.53c62f80f931.

14. Hartford Community Loan Fund, https://www.hartfordloans.org/.

15. Frank O'Gorman, "Faith—Politics—Revolution!" http://frankogorman .tumblr.com/.

Chapter 1: Understanding the Struggles for LGBTQ Equality and Racial Justice

1. This acronym also includes those who identify their sexuality in still other ways, including asexual, gender fluid, genderqueer, and more.

2. Claire Ainsworth, "Sex Redefined," *International Weekly Journal of Science 518*, no. 7539 (February 18, 2009), http://www.nature.com/news/sex -redefined-1.16943.

3. "What Scientists Know—and Don't Know—about Sexual Orientation," *Association for Psychological Science*, April 25, 2016, http://www .psychologicalscience.org/index.php/news/releases/what-scientists-know -and-don't-know-about-sexual-orientation.html.

4. Mark D. Jordan, *The Invention of Sodomy in Christian Theology* (Chicago: University of Chicago Press, 1997), 169.

5. Thanks to Elana Keppel Levy for this insight. The term "homosexuality" emerged in the nineteenth-century medicine as a diagnostic and classifying term. See Jordan, *Invention of Sodomy in Christian Theology*, 161. See also Jeffrey Weeks, *Sex, Politics, and the Society: The Regulation of Sexuality since 1800*, 2nd ed. (London: Longman Ltd., 1989), 21.

6. James H. Evans Jr., *We Have Been Believers* (Minneapolis: Fortress Press, 1992), 35.

7. "Federal Appeals Court Upholds Students' Rights in Gay-Straight Alliance Case," American Civil Liberties Union of Florida, https://aclufl .org/2016/12/06/federal-appeals-court-upholds-students-rights-in-gay -straight-alliance-case/.

Jennifer Toomer-Cook and Marjorie Cortez, "3 Groups Sue S. L. Board over Clubs," Deseret News, http:www.deseretnews.com/article/619419/3 -groups-sue-SL-board-over-clubs.html; Kate Royals, "Proposed LGBT Club Prompts New Rankin School Policy," the *Clarion-Ledger*, http:www .clarionledger.com/story/news/local/2015/01/rankin-schools-gay-club -policy/21745481/.

8. "Frequently Asked Questions about GSA Network," GSA Network, https:// gsanetwork.org/about-us/faq.

9. Sacred Congregation for the Doctrine of the Faith, "Persona Humana: Declaration on Certain Questions concerning Sexual Ethics," http://www .vatican.va/roman_curia/congregations/cfaith/documents/rc_con_cfaith _doc_19751229_persona-humana_en.html.

10. The extent of antidiscrimination protection varies by state, and some states that forbid discrimination based on sexual orientation allow it for transgenderism. See "Non-Discrimination Laws," Movement Advancement Project (August 29, 2016), http://www.lgbtmap.org/equality-maps/non _discrimination_laws.

11. Emily Waters, Chai Jindasurat, and Cecilia Wolfe, "National Report on Hate Violence against Lesbian, Gay, Bisexual, Transgender, Queer, and HIV-Affected Communities Released Today," National Coalition of Anti-Violence Programs (June 14, 2016), http://avp.org/wp-content /uploads/2017/06/2016_NCAVP_HateViolence_Report.pdf.

12. Transracial adoption adds layers of complication to this reality because it creates families in which individuals may have distinct racial identities, which can then be passed on to the next generation. The presence of variously racially identified individuals has implications for how the family as a whole identifies itself and is identified by others.

13. This is often not the case for transracial adoptees.

14. "Frequently Asked Questions about GSA Network," GSA Network, https://gsanetwork.org/about-us/faq.

15. Willie James Jennings, *The Christian Imagination: Theology and the Origins of Race* (New Haven: Yale University Press, 2010), 64.

16. Cheryl I. Harris, "Whiteness as Property," *Harvard Law Review* 106, no. 8 (June 1993), 1715. Harris writes, "The racialization of identity and the racial subordination of Blacks and Native Americans provided the ideological basis for slavery and conquest."

17. See David R. Roediger, *The Wages of Whiteness: Race and the Making of the American Working Class* (London: Verso, 1991), 24. Roediger notes that between 1600 and 1800, racial lines were often blurred among the poor.

18. Harris, "Whiteness as Property," 17–18. See also "Interview with James O. Horton," PBS.org, 2003, http://www.pbs.org/race/000_About/002_04 -background-02-04.htm. See also Jennifer Harvey, *Dear White Christians: For Those Still Longing for Racial Reconciliation* (Grand Rapids, MI: Eerdmans, 2014), 47–52. Harvey focuses on different moments within the same historical process, including the emergence of the word "negro."

19. This text was originally published in 1843 under the title, *Slavery, As It Relates to the Negro, or African Race*. It was renamed in revised editions published in the 1850s.

20. Mark Galli, "Slaveholding Evangelist: Whitefield's Troubling Mix of Views," *Christianity Today*, http://www.christianitytoday.com/history/issues /issue-38/slaveholding-evangelist.html.

21. Eric Foner, "Rooted in Reconstruction: The First Wave of Black Congressmen," *The Nation* (October 15, 2008), http://www.thenation.com/article /rooted-reconstruction-first-wave-black-congressmen/.

22. Elizabeth Anderson and Jeffrey Jones, "Race, Voting Rights, and Segregation: Rise and Fall of the Black Voter, 1868–1922; The End of Reconstruction, 1879," The Geography of Race in the U.S., University of Michigan (September 2002), http://umich.edu/~lawrace/votetour4.htm.

23. "Black Code and Jim Crow Law Examples," Central Piedmont Community College (December 2, 2009), https://sites.google.com/a/email.cpcc.edu /black-codes-and-jim-crow/black-code-and-jim-crow-law-examples.

24. Douglas A. Blackmon, *Slavery by Another Name: The Re-enslavement of Black People in America from the Civil War to World War II* (New York: Doubleday, 2008), 53–57, 117–54, 270–98.

25. Matthew S. Mendez and Christian R. Grose, "Doubling Down: Inequality in Responsiveness and the Policy Preferences of Elected Officials," Social Science Research Network, University of Southern California (May 1, 2014), http://ssrn.com/abstract=2422596.

26. According to *Lynching in America: Confronting the Legacy of Racial Terror* (Montgomery, AL: Equal Justice Initiative, 2015), 3,959 African Americans were lynched in the South between 1877 and 1950.

27. James Allen, John Lewis, Leon F. Litwack, and Hilton Als, *Without Sanctuary: Lynching Photography in America* (Santa Fe: Twin Palms, 2000).

28. James Allen and John Littlefield, "Without Sanctuary: Photographs and Postcards of Lynching in America," 2000–2005, http://withoutsanctuary .org/main.html.

29. "[M]any African Americans who were never accused of any crime were tortured and murdered in front of picnicking spectators (including elected officials and prominent citizens) for bumping into a white person, or wearing their military uniforms after World War I, or not using the appropriate title when addressing a white person. People who participated in lynchings were celebrated and acted with impunity." See Equal Justice Initiative, "Lynching in America: Confronting the Legacy of Racial Terror," http://www.eji.org /lynchinginamerica.

30. "United States v. Bhagat Singh Thind, 261 U.S. 204 (1923)" *Justia*, U.S. Supreme Court, https://supreme.justia.com/cases/federal/us/261/204/case .html.

31. Harris, "Whiteness as Property."

32. Larry DeWitt, "The Decision to Exclude Agricultural and Domestic Workers from the 1935 Social Security Act," Social Security Office of Disability and Retirement Policy, *Social Security Bulletin* 70, no. 4 (2010), https://www .ssa.gov/policy/docs/ssb/v70n4/v70n4p49.html.

33. Jack Dougherty, "Home Owners Loan Corporation (HOLC) Residential Security 'Redlining' Map and Area Descriptions," On the Line research project, University of Connecticut, http://magic.lib.uconn.edu/magic_2 /vector/37840/primary_source/hdimg_37840_064_1937_holc_national _archives_trinity.pdf.

34. Ira Katznelson, *When Affirmative Action Was White: An Untold History of Racial Inequality in Twentieth Century America* (New York: W. W. Norton and Company, Inc., 2005), 140–41.

35. See the work of Bryan Stevenson of the Equal Justice Initiative at http://

www.eji.org and Michele Alexander, *The New Jim Crow: Mass Incarceration in the Age of Color Blindness* (New York: New Press, 2010).
36. Dan Baum, "Legalize It All," *Harper's Magazine* (April 2016), https://harpers.org/archive/2016/04/legalize-it-all/.
37. United States Department of Justice Civil Rights Division, "Department of Justice Report on the Ferguson, Mo. Police Department," *The Washington Post* (March 4, 2015), http://apps.washingtonpost.com/g/documents/national/department-of-justice-report-on-the-ferguson-mo-police-department/1435/.
38. Mark Berman and Wesley Lowery, "The 12 Key Highlights from the DOJ's Scathing Ferguson Report," *The Washington Post* (March 4, 2015), https://www.washingtonpost.com/news/post-nation/wp/2015/03/04/the-12-key-highlights-from-the-dojs-scathing-ferguson-report/.
39. Jonathan Rothwell, "How the War on Drugs Damages Black Social Mobility," Brookings Institution, https://www.brookings.edu/blog/social-mobility-memos/2014/09/30/how-the-war-on-drugs-damages-black-social-mobility/. See also "Criminal Justice Fact Sheet," NAACP, http://www.naacp.org/pages/criminal-justice-fact-sheet.
40. Judith Greene, Kevin Pranis, and Jason Ziedenberg, "Disparity by Design: How Drug-Free Zone Laws Impact Racial Disparity—and Fail to Protect Youth," Justice Policy Institute (March, 2006), http://www.google.com/url?url=http://www.justicepolicy.org/uploads/justicepolicy/documents/06-03_rep_disparitybydesign_dp-jj-rd.pdf&rct=j&q=&esrc=s&sa=U&ved=0ahUKEwj25YPfh9XLAhVY2GMKHWn-CM4QFggUMAA&usg=AFQjCNH-yjn1CwIAn8FpD9i-PWhna0amhA.
41. Joseph J. Plamar, Shelby Davies, Danielle C. Ompad, Charles M. Cleland, and Michael Weitzman, "Powder Cocaine and Crack Use in the United States: An examination of risk for arrest and socioeconomic disparities in use," *Drug and Alcohol Dependence*, April 2015, vol. 148, 108–116, http://www.drugandalcoholdependence.com/article/S0376-8716(15)00049-6/abstract.
42. Gary Stewart, "Black Codes and Broken Windows: the Legacy of Racial Hegemony in Anti-Gang Civil Injunctions," *Yale Law Journal*, May 98, vol. 107, no. 7, 2249–279, http://connection.ebscohost.com/c/articles/689372/black-codes-broken-windows-legacy-racial.
43. Department of Justice Office of Public Affairs, "Justice Department Announces Findings of Investigation into Baltimore Police Department," The United States Department of Justice (August 10, 2016), https://www.justice.gov/opa/pr/justice-department-announces-findings-investigation-baltimore-police-department.

44. Besiki Kutateladze, Whitney Tymas, and Mary Crowley, "Race and Prosecution in Manhattan," Vera Institute of Justice (July 2014), http://www.vera.org/pubs/special/race-and-prosecution-manhattan. Lindsey Devers, "Plea and Charge Bargaining Research Summary," Bureau of Justice Assistance: U.S. Department of Justice (January 24, 2011), https://www.google.com/url?q=https://www.bja.gov/Publications/PleaBargaining ResearchSummary.pdf&sa=U&ved=0ahUKEwjG_brKi9XLAhXC2T 4KHQLrDYUQFggeMAE&usg=AFQjCNFCAcrpnIhTNZUn 6Lfzw99IDhTaTg.

45. Gene Demby, "Study Reveals Worse Outcomes for Black and Latino Defendants," NPR Code Switch (July 17, 2014), http://www.npr.org/sections/codeswitch/2014/07/17/332075947/study-reveals-worse-outcomes-for-black-and-latino-defendants.

46. Devah Pager, *Marked: Race, Crime, and Finding Work in an Era of Mass Incarceration* (Chicago: University of Chicago Press, 2009), 93, 154–55.

47. Brent Staples, "The Racist Origins of Felon Disenfranchisement," *New York Times* (November 18, 2014), http://www.nytimes.com/2014/11/19/opinion/the-racist-origins-of-felon-disenfranchisement.html. See also "Felony Disenfranchisement," The Sentencing Project (2016), http://www.sentencingproject.org/template/page.cfm?id=133.

48. "The Eight Mile Wall," Detroiturbex, http://detroiturbex.com/content/neighborhoods/8milewall/index.html.

49. Emily Badger and Darla Cameron, "How Railroads, Highways and other Man-Made Lines Racially Divide America's Cities," *The Washington Post* (July 16, 2015), https://www.washingtonpost.com/news/wonk/wp/2015/07/16/how-railroads-highways-and-other-man-made-lines-racially-divide-americas-cities/.

50. Elizabeth Anderson and Jeffrey Jones, "Causes of Housing Segregation," The Geography of Race in the U.S., University of Michigan (September 2002), http://www.umich.edu/~lawrace/causes1.htm.

51. "Transcript of Brown v. Board of Education (1954)," Our Documents Initiative, *https://www.ourdocuments.gov/doc.php?flash=true&doc=87&page=transcript.*

52. See https://www.ibiblio.org/sncc/white_lib.html. See also Charles Marsh, *God's Long Summer: Stories of Faith and Civil Rights* (Princeton, NJ: Princeton University Press 1997), 182.

53. Julian Bond, "SNCC: What We Did," *Monthly Review: An Independent Socialist Magazine*, http://monthlyreview.org/2000/10/01/sncc-what-we-did/.

54. Harris, "Whiteness as Property."

55. "Huey P. Newton on Gay, Women's Liberation," *Workers World* (May 16, 2012), http://www.workers.org/2012/us/huey_p_newton_0524/.

Chapter 2: Getting Ready to Be an Ally

1. Samuel Wells, *Improvisation: The Drama of Christian Ethics* (Grand Rapids: Brazos Press, 2004), 75.
2. Letty M. Russell, *The Future of Partnership* (Louisville, KY: Westminster John Knox Press, 1979), 157.
3. Karl Rahner, *The Love of Jesus and the Love of Neighbor* (New York: Crossroad, 1983), 71.
4. Friedrich Schleiermacher, *The Christian Faith* (New York: Harper & Row, 1963), 288.
5. See Jim Wallis, *America's Original Sin: Racism, White Privilege, and the Bridge to a New America* (Grand Rapids: Brazos Press, 2016). See also Harvey, *Dear White Christians*, 201.
6. H. Richard Niebuhr, *The Responsible Self: An Essay in Christian Moral Philosophy* (New York: Harper & Row, 1963), 133.
7. This is a phrase used often by theologian Marilyn McCord Adams, who was also one of the activist advisors for this project.
8. Harvey, *Dear White Christians*, 46–47.
9. Ta-Nehisi Coates, "The Case for Reparations," *The Atlantic*, June 2014, http://tehatlantic.com/magazine/archive/2014/06/the-case-for-reparations/361631
10. Quoted in Harvey, *Dear White Christians*, 119.
11. Ibid.
12. Ibid., 121.
13. Coates, *Between the World and Me*, 24–25.
14. Ibid., 64.
15. Harvey, *Dear White Christians*, 253.

Chapter 3: Resources for Being an Ally

1. Janet Martin Soskice, "The Ends of and the Future of God," in *The End of the World and the Ends of God: Science and Theology on Eschatology*, eds. John Polkinghorne and Michael Welker (Harrisburg, PA: Trinity Press International, 2000), 86.
2. Thanks to Robert Merrihew Adams for this phrasing.
3. Hartford Community Loan Fund, https://www.hartfordloans.org/.
4. Plato, *The Republic* (Cambridge, MA: Harvard University Press, 1969–70).
5. This comment came from the Sixth Annual Center on Race and Inequality King Justice Lecture, given by Rev. Osagyefo Sekou at the University of Louisville on January 21, 2015.
6. M., "A Critique of Ally Politics," in *Taking Sides: Revolutionary Solidarity and the Poverty of Liberalism*, ed. Cindy Milstein (Oakland, CA: AK Press, 2016), 67.
7. Emphasis added.

Chapter 4: Concrete Steps

1. Eric Lipton, "With No Warning, House Republicans Vote to Gut Independent Ethics Office," *New York Times*, January 2, 2017, http://nytimes.com/2017/01/02/us/politics/with-no-warning-house-republicans-vote-to-hobble-independent-ethics-office.html.
2. Eric Lipton and Matt Flegenheimer, "House Republicans, Under Fire, Back Down on Gutting Ethics Office," *New York Times*, January 3, 2017, http://www.nytimes.com/2017/01/03/us/politics/trump-house-ethics-office.html?_r=0.
3. Ben Mathis-Lilley, "Hey, A Bunch of People Called Their Representatives in Congress, and It Actually Worked!" *Slate*, January 3, 2017, http://www.slate.com/blogs/the_slatest/2017/01/03/reps_say_phone_calls_prompted_ethics_reversal.html
4. David Hartsough and Joyce Hollyday, *Waging Peace: Global Adventures of a Lifelong Activist* (Oakland, CA: PM Press, 2014), 115.
5. Miguel De La Torre, *The Politics of Jesús: A Hispanic Political Theology* (Lanham, MD: Rowan and Littlefield, 2015), 160.
6. Colleen Flaherty, "Being Watched," *Inside Higher Ed*, November 22, 2016, https://www.insidehighered.com/news/2016/11/22/new-website-seeks-register-professors-accused-liberal-bias-and-anti-american-values.
7. Professor Watchlist, http://professorwatchlist.org.
8. Marion Grau, "'The Camp Is a Ceremony': A Report from Standing Rock," *Religion Dispatches*, November 25, 2016, http://religiondispatches.org/decolonizing-thanksgiving-at-standing-rock-a-black-friday-report/.

Chapter 5: Examples to Follow

1. See Brian Bantum, *Redeeming Mulatto: A Theology of Race and Christian Identity* (Waco, TX: Baylor University Press, 2010).
2. Myles Horton and Paulo Freire, *We Make the Road by Walking: Conversations on Education and Social Change*, ed. Brenda Bell, John Gaventa, and John M. Peters (Philadelphia: Temple University Press, 1990), 177.
3. Kristina Lindgren, "Myles Horton, 84: Founder of Early Civil Rights Center," *Los Angeles Times*, http://articles.latimes.com/1990-01-21/news/mn-757_1_myles-horton.
4. "Myles Horton (1905–1990)," StateUniversity.com, http://education.stateuniversity.com/pages/2072/Horton-Myles-1905-1990.html.
5. John Davis, "Myles Horton: The Radical Hillbilly," UAW Region 8 Activist Hall of Fame, http://www.uawregion8.net/Activist-HOF/M-Horton.htm.
6. Ibid.
7. "Myles Horton (1905–1990)."

8. Kenneth Torquil MacLean, "Origins of the Southern Civil Rights Movement: Myles Horton and the Highlander Folk School," *The Phi Delta Kappan* 47, no. 9, 487–89, http://www.jstor.org/stable/20371644.
9. "Myles Horton," Adult Learning Unleashed, http://www.alu-c.com/myles-horton/.
10. "Myles Horton," http://onevotesncc.org/profile/myles-horton/.
11. Ibid.
12. Dale Jacobs, ed., *The Myles Horton Reader: Education for Social Change* (Knoxville, TN: University of Tennessee Press, 2003), xxviii.
13. Davis, "Myles Horton: The Radical Hillbilly."
14. Robert Shetterly, "Ann Braden," Americans Who Tell the Truth: Models of Courageous Citizenship, http://www.americanswhotellthetruth.org/portraits/anne-braden.
15. Catherine Fosl, *Subversive Southerner: Anne Braden and the Struggle for Racial Justice in the Cold War South* (Lexington, KY: University Press of Kentucky, 2006), 198.
16. Catherine Fosl, "Braden, Anne," American National Biography Online, http://www.anb.org/articles/15/15-01366.html.
17. Anne Braden, "A Letter to White Southern Women from Anne Braden" (Louisville, KY: SCEF Press, 1972), http://www.newsreel.org/guides/Anne-Braden-Southern-Patriot-Resources/Anne-Braden-A-Letter-to-White-Southern-Women.pdf.
18. Ibid.
19. Ibid.
20. Ibid.
21. Ibid.
22. Ibid.
23. "Anne Braden: Southern Patriot," Kentucky Alliance Against Racist and Political Oppression and the Carl Braden Memorial Center, http://annebradenfilm.org/stories.
24. Ibid.
25. "Who Was Anne Braden?" Anne Braden Institute for Social Justice Research, http://louisville.edu/braden/about/who-was-anne-braden.
26. Rev. James Martin, SJ, "Jeanne Manford, Founder of PFLAG, Loved Prophetically," *The Huffington Post* (March 11, 2013), http://www.huffingtonpost.com/rev-james-martin-sj/jeanne-manford-pflag_b_2439839.html.
27. Ibid.
28. Jeanne Manford, "Letter to the Editor," *New York Post* (April 29, 1972), also quoted in Martin, "Jeanne Manford."
29. Martin, "Jeanne Manford."

30. Ibid.
31. Lily Percy, "Jeanne Manford: A Mother First, Gay Rights Activist Second," NPR, All Things Considered (January 12, 2013), http://www.npr.org/2013/01/12/169223070/remembering-pflag-founder-and-mother.
32. Kat Michels, "Heroines of History: Jeanne Manford—The Mother of the Straight Ally Movement," *Business Heroine Magazine* (May 28, 2015), http://businessheroinemagazine.com/jeannemanford/.
33. PFLAG.org, https://www.pflag.org/blog/letterdearabby.
34. PFLAG.org, https://www.pflag.org/proudpeople, see "Our Priorities."
35. "PFLAG.org, https://www.pflag.org/diverse-inclusive-world.
36. Rebecca Trounson, "Jeanne Manford Dies at 92; Co-founder of Group for Parents of Gays," *Los Angeles Times* (January 10, 2013), http://www.latimes.com/local/obituaries/la-me-jeanne-manford-20130110-story.html.
37. "Obituary: Jeanne Manford/Co-founder of Group for Parents of Gays," *PittsburghPost-Gazette* (January 12, 2013), http://www.post-gazette.com/news/obituaries/2013/01/12/Obituary-Jeanne-Manford-Co-founder-of-group-for-parents-of-gays/stories/201301120183.
38. Katrina Browne, "Confronting Slavery in the Deep North," *The Root* (June 20, 2008), http://www.theroot.com/articles/culture/2008/06/confronting_slavery_in_the_deep_north/.
39. Public Allies, http://publicallies.org/#section-our-mission.
40. Ibid.
41. Pleun Bouricius, "Traces of the Trade: An Interview with Filmmaker Katrina Browne," *Mass Humanities* (Spring 2008), http://masshumanities.org/about/news/s08-tot/.
42. A notable exception to this is Howard Zinn, *A People's History of the United States: 1492–2001* (New York: HarperCollins, 2003).
43. "History of the State of Rhode Island and Providence Plantations: Biographical," *Rootsweb*, The USGenWeb Project, accessed August 31, 2016, http://www.rootsweb.ancestry.com/~rigenweb/articles/210.html.
44. "Traces of the Trade: A Story of the Deep North," http://www.tracesofthetrade.org/.
45. Frederick Douglass, "The Meaning of July Fourth for the Negro," PBS, http://www.pbs.org/wgbh/aia/part4/4h2927t.html.
46. "Get Involved," http://www.tracesofthetrade.org/get-involved/.
47. Bouricius, "Traces of the Trade," http://masshumanities.org/about/news/s08-tot/.
48. Browne attributes this to Jean-Jacques Rousseau. Katrina Browne, "Commentary: Slavery Needs More Than an Apology," CNN (August 19, 2008) http://www.cnn.com/2009/POLITICS/08/19/browne.slavery/.

For Further Study

Alexander, Michelle. *The New Jim Crow: Mass Incarceration in the Age of Colorblindness.* New York: New Press, 2011.

Bantum, Brian. *Redeeming Mulatto: A Theology of Race and Christian Hybridity.* Waco, TX: Baylor University Press, 2010.

Barber, William J., II, with Jonathan Wilson-Hartgrove. *The Third Reconstruction: Moral Mondays, Fusion Politics, and the Rise of a New Justice Movement.* Boston: Beacon Press, 2016.

Beyond the Pale: Reading Theology from the Margins. Edited by De La Torre, Miquel A. and Stacey M. Floyd-Thomas. Louisville, KY: Westminster John Knox, 2011.

Blackmon, Douglas A. *Slavery by Another Name: The Re-enslavement of Black People in America from the Civil War to World War II.* New York: Doubleday, 2008.

Brooks, Adrian. *The Right Side of History: 100 Years of LGBTQ Activism.* New York: Cleis Press, 2015.

Coates, Ta-Nehisi. *Between the World and Me.* New York: Spiegel and Grau, 2015.

Coleman, Arica L. *That the Blood Stay Pure: African Americans, Native Americans, and the Predicament of Race and Identity in Virginia.* Blacks in the Diaspora. Bloomington: Indiana University Press, 2013.

Collins, Patricia Hill and Sirma Bilge. *Intersectionality. Key Concepts.* Malden, MA: Polity Press, 2016.

Cone, James H. *Martin and Malcolm and America: A Dream or a Nightmare.* Maryknoll, NY: Orbis Books, 2000.

Cottrell, Susan. *"Mom, I'm Gay": Loving Your LGBTQ Child and Strengthening Your Faith.* Revised and Expanded Edition. Louisville, KY: Westminster John Knox Press, 2016.

De La Torre, Miquel A. *The Politics of Jesús: A Hispanic Political Theology.* Lanham, MD: Rowman and Littlefield, 2015.

Douglas, Kelly Brown. *Stand Your Ground: Black Bodies and the Justice of God.* Maryknoll, NY: Orbis Books, 2015.

Dunbar-Ortiz, Roxanne. *An Indigenous Peoples' History of the United States.* Boston: Beacon Press, 2014.

Farley, Margaret. *Just Love.* New York: Continuum International Publishing Group, 2006.

Francis, Leah Gunning. *Ferguson and Faith: Sparking Leadership and Awakening Community.* St. Louis: Chalice Press, 2015.

Gonzalez, Juan. *Harvest of Empire: A History of Latinos in America.* New York: Penguin Books, 2000.

Harvey, Jennifer. *Dear White Christians: For Those Still Longing for Racial Reconciliation.* Grand Rapids, MI: Eerdmans Publishing, 2014.

Jarecki, Eugene, Melinda Shopsin, Nannie Jeter, David Simon, Sam Cullman, Derek Hallquist, Robert Miller, and Paul Frost. *The House I Live In.* New York: Charlotte Street Films, 2012.

Jennings, Willie James. *The Christian Imagination: Theology and the Origins of Race.* New Haven, CT: Yale University Press, 2010.

López, Ian Haney. *White by Law: The Legal Construction of Race.* 10th Anniversary Edition. New York: New York University Press, 2006.

Martin, Colby. *UnClobber: Rethinking Our Misuse of the Bible on Homosexuality.* Louisville, KY: Westminster John Knox Press, 2016.

Molina, Natalia. *How Race Is Made in America: Immigration, Citizenship, and the Historical Power of Racial Scripts.* Berkeley: University of California Press, 2014.

Off the Menu: Asian and Asian North American Women's Religion and Theology. Edited by Jung Ha Kim, Kwok Pui Lan, Rita Nakashima Brock, and Seung Ai Yang. Louisville, KY: Westminster John Knox Press, 2007.

Pounder, CCH, Larry Adelman, Jean Cheng, Christine Herbes-Sommers, Tracy H. Strain, Llewellyn Smith, and Claudio Ragazzi. *Race: The Power of an Illusion*. San Francisco: California Newsreel, 2003. See also www.pbs.org/race.

Rodríguez, Rubén Rosario. *Racism and God-Talk: A Latino/a Perspective*. New York: New York University Press, 2008.

Roediger, David R. *The Wages of Whiteness: Race and the Making of the American Working Class*. London: Verso, 1991.

Rogers, Jack. *Jesus, the Bible, and Homosexuality*. Revised and Expanded Edition. Louisville, KY: Westminster John Knox Press, 2009.

Tatum, Beverly Daniel. *"Why Are All the Black Kids Sitting Together in the Cafeteria?" and Other Conversations about Race*. New York: Basic Books, 1997.

Thurman, Howard. *Jesus and the Disinherited*. Nashville, TN: Abingdon Press, 1949.

Townes, Emilie M. *Womanist Ethics and the Cultural Production of Evil*. New York: Palgrave Macmillan, 2006.

Viefhues-Bailey, Ludger H. *Between a Man and a Woman: Why Conservatives Oppose Same-Sex Marriage*. New York: Columbia University Press, 2010.

Wallis, Jim. *America's Original Sin: Racism, White Privilege, and the Bridge to a New America*. Grand Rapids, MI: Brazos Press, 2016.

Washington, Harriet A. *Medical Apartheid: The Dark History of Medical Experimentation on Black Americans from Colonial Times to the Present*. New York: Doubleday, 2006.

Wiesner-Hanks, Merry E. *Gender in History: Global Perspectives*. Malden: Blackwell Publishing, 2011.

Wu, Frank. *Yellow: Race in America between Black and White*. New York: Basic Books, 2002.

Acknowledgments

I humbly acknowledge the many teachers I've had in this life who have shared their knowledge with me in the pursuit of wisdom: in particular, my parents, Angela and Charles Doucot; David J. O'Brien from the College of the Holy Cross; Claire and Scott Schaeffer-Duffy of the Saints Francis and Therese Catholic Worker community of Worcester, Massachusetts; and my many friends from the north end of Hartford who showed me the difference between charity and justice and continue to inspire me to seek a world of peace with justice, justice with mercy, and life with dignity for all of God's children.

—Chris Doucot

The people who have taught me the most about racism and heterosexism and the need to struggle against these forms of oppression have been students. To every student who took the time and energy to teach and mentor me, I give thanks. I am grateful to the communities at Louisville Seminary and Crescent Hill Presbyterian Church, who have supported me in this work. Phillips Seminary and First Presbyterian Church of Sarasota graciously afforded me opportunities to develop some of the ideas in this volume. Marilyn McCord Adams, Lewis Brogdon, Jennifer Ho, Tyler Mayfield, and Tom Zoellner kindly offered comments on parts of the manuscript. David Lott helped give shape to the whole, while Elana Keppel Levy prevented several linguistic catastrophes. This book would never have been written without the encouragement and guidance of Robert Ratcliff.

I give thanks to my friends who held me close during the writing of this text as I struggled with hard realities, my own ignorance, and the vulnerability required to do this work. Finally, I am grateful to and for my family—Seth, Jacob, Elias, and Lucy— who teach me hope and bring me joy.

—Shannon Craigo-Snell

The authors' royalties from the sale of this book will be donated to efforts to promote LGBTQ equality and racial justice.

CPSIA information can be obtained
at www.ICGtesting.com
Printed in the USA
FSOW02n1610280917
39250FS

9 780664 262624